Mourning
with Those
Who Mourn

Mourning with Those Who Mourn

Edited by

STEVEN C. WALKER & JANE D. BRADY

BOOKCRAFT
SALT LAKE CITY, UTAH

Library of Congress Catalog Card Number: 99-72162

ISBN 1-57008-626-5

First Printing, 1999

Printed in the United States of America

In Memory of Our Mothers:
Marian Joy Crockett Brereton
and
Elaine DeGraff Walker

CONTENTS

INTRODUCTION

One of the happiest aspects of being Latter-day Saints is our sure feeling of hereafters. Death is for us not the final tragedy it is for most people—death for us is less a termination than a temporary interruption in our earthly relationships. In our Mormon communities we remind ourselves frequently that people do not so much die as go on missions to better places. We anticipate little of the "sore havoc" that Robert Louis Stevenson sees in death; we don't expect "the changes wrought by death" to be "so sharp and final, and so terrible and melancholy in their consequences."[1]

Therefore when death comes to us, inevitably as sunset follows dawn, we can be caught by surprise that it hurts so much. We are shocked that the people who die—our parents, our spouses, our children—are not theoretically passed away but actually and irretrievably dead. We were moved to write this book because we miss our dead parents more profoundly than we thought we might. We find we're not alone in that. Talking with others about their experiences with death has convinced us that death is an experience Latter-day Saints share with others too little. It is an experience we would be the better for sharing. "Grief remains one of the few things that has the power to silence us. It is a whisper in the world and a clamor within. . . . Even more than its usher death, grief is unspoken, publicly ignored except for those moments at the funeral that are over too quickly."[2]

We are so certain in our culture of eventual eternities that the present reality of death can blindside us. We do not know how to grieve. Not expecting to mourn, we have not trained ourselves in the process:

> Everybody knows they're going to die, . . . but nobody believes it. If we did, we would do things differently.
>
> So we kid ourselves about death. . . .

> But there's a better approach. To know you're going to die, and to be prepared for it at any time. That's better. That way you can actually be more involved in your life while you're living.[3]

Our hope here is to help Latter-day Saints be more alive to death, more "willing to mourn with those that mourn; yea, and comfort those that stand in need of comfort . . . even until death" (Mosiah 18:9). Our hope is to help us as a people mourn better, to honor the lives of our loved ones and to reach resolution in our relationships in such spiritually nurturing ways that "all they who have mourned shall be comforted" (D&C 101:14). This book has in it practical guides to grieving—it is something of a handbook of constructive ways to mourn, of helpful means of finding comfort.

These how-to-approach-death suggestions grow out of hard-earned experience with dying; they are heartfelt rather than theoretical. Each essay is a personal testimony of what works and what doesn't work. These are testimonies that bloom from the writers' direct dealings with death. Fourteen Latter-day Saint essayists with widely different perspectives on death—one having undergone the death more than twenty years ago, one within the past year—share their insights into how best to cope with dying. This broad range of personal experiences provides a kaleidoscope of views on different kinds of death, creating a rich spectrum of possibilities for how you might best deal with death in your life.

The last thing we want to do is explain your grief away. We are painfully aware that we do not understand your grief any more than you understand ours. There is something private in grief, something that feels insulted when someone says "I know how you feel. When my dog died. . . ." The commonness of death does not make it any easier for any of us. Even the orphan who has watched all his loved ones die in grievous ways is no expert on the deaths we must go through—there remains something intensely personal about death, something special about our own dyings.

So we have no sure recipes for positive grieving. As these essays testify, every death is different, every experience with death unique. No one can "do death" once and for all; all of us must deal with dying on a case-by-case basis. But though there are no surefire formulas, there are solid suggestions in this book, practical things you might do that have worked for other people confronted with death, concrete approaches that could prove helpful for you in your own mourning.

Beyond that you should find in the book uncanny comfort. In the worst of human tragedies we seem to be at our best when we share, when we open ourselves to the reality of our own suffering and the suffering of our friends. Grief shared is love expanded, pain divided. We have been vastly comforted by these accounts of the ways good people have dealt with death. We hope you will be similarly comforted as you struggle with these writers through the process of grieving. Personal as the process is, death, like love, feels better shared.

People wonder why we're so fascinated with something as morbid as death—why write a book about grieving? What we are really interested in, in our lives and in this book, is life. Death matters only because it is so crucial an aspect of our living. "The meaning of life is connected, inextricably, to the meaning of death . . . mourning is a romance in reverse, and if you love, you grieve and there are no exceptions—only those who do it well and those who don't. And if death is regarded as an embarrassment or an inconvenience, if the dead are regarded as a nuisance from whom we seek a hurried riddance, then life and the living are in for like treatment."[4]

He who lived and died for us assured us: "I am come that they might have life, and that they might have it more abundantly" (John 10:10). Death is a part of that abundance, a part we hope this book will enable you to enjoy more fully, more satisfyingly. Death can be a transforming experience, and not only for those who die, as can be seen from the experience of one journalist: "My father's death forever changed my relationship to life. Sitting at his bedside when his breathing stopped, I was awed by the transformations in his body: the deep relaxation that smoothed his furrowed brow, the look of pained concentration that slowly changed to wonder, the pearly translucence that radiated softly around him. I felt that I was witnessing a sacred event, perhaps even a miracle."[5]

There is in death something miraculous, something enlivening that those who have experienced want to share. May these heartfelt testimonies of death help you deal with death more fulfillingly. May they help you share your grief and embrace the grief of others. May they make you, as they have made us, more fully alive. May these essays enable you to come to know something of what President Hinckley knows of death and the life it mirrors: "I also came to know something of death—the absolute devastation of children losing their mother—but also of peace without pain and the certainty that death cannot be the end of the soul."[6]

—Steve Walker and Jane Brady

Notes

1. Robert Louis Stevenson, "ÆS Triplex," *Selected Poetry and Prose of Robert Louis Stevenson*, ed. Bradford A. Booth (Boston: Houghton Mifflin Company, 1968), p. 11.

2. Anna Quindlen, "Grief lives on as a universal silencer," *Deseret News*, May 8, 1994, p. S4.

3. Mitch Albom, *Tuesdays with Morrie* (New York: Doubleday, 1997), p. 81.

4. Thomas Lynch, *The Undertaking* (New York: W. W. Norton & Company, 1997), p. 25.

5. Pithia Peay, "Mastering the Natural Art of Dying," *UTNE Reader*, March–April, 1998, p. 68.

6. Gordon B. Hinckley, "Some Lessons I Learned As a Boy," *Ensign*, May 1993, p. 54.

CIRCLES AND SPIRALS: EMOTIONAL RESPONSES TO LOSS

by Jay Fox

IN GRIEF NOTHING "STAYS PUT." ONE KEEPS ON EMERGING FROM A PHASE, BUT IT ALWAYS RECURS. ROUND AND ROUND. EVERYTHING REPEATS. AM I GOING IN CIRCLES, OR DARE I HOPE I AM ON A SPIRAL?

—C. S. LEWIS

Grieving is neither a single nor a static emotional response to loss. Those of us who experience grief know that many changing feelings are involved. Grief counselors often arrange these feelings into "stages." One of the most well-known thanatologists is Elisabeth Kübler-Ross, whose *On Death and Dying* set forth five stages: denial and isolation, anger, bargaining, depression, and acceptance.[1] The 1988 edition of the LDS *Relief Society Handbook* encourages Relief Society presidents to "be aware of stages of grief. There are stages of grief that most people go through when they have a severe crisis. Understanding these stages may help you understand the sister, and the sister may find it useful to know that her reactions are normal."[2] The handbook identifies four stages: shock and denial, anger, depression, and acceptance. In the current bestseller, *Spontaneous Healing*, medical doctor Andrew Weil describes a similar list but adds a "wishful fantasy" stage between

---

***Jay Fox** and his wife, Dawn Webb, are the parents of six children and are teacher trainers for the Family-to-Family Education Program sponsored by the National Alliance for the Mentally Ill. Jay chairs the Utah State Board of Mental Health and is a professor of English at Brigham Young University. He is the high priests group leader in his ward.*

"anger and rage" and depression. He qualifies his description by suggesting the stages "may or may not occur sequentially" and that "perhaps it would be better to call them facets of grief rather than stages."[3]

Although other professionals, such as Kenneth J. Doka in his *Living with Grief: Who We Are, How We Grieve*, encourage "a move away from such approaches, which tend to homogenize the processing of grief,"[4] the stages approach is still widely used and effective in helping us understand our grief. Doka's concern is that the stages "imply that all individuals, irrespective of their many differences, will grieve in a similar way."[5] He urges us to keep in mind the individual differences and circumstances of those dealing with death, especially the variables of "age, gender, developmental level, social class, cultural and religious beliefs and practices, family, and external and internal support."[6] If we team up the stages approach with sensitivity for individual responses in a cultural context such as Doka promotes, the two approaches can become powerful allies.

One of the most useful and complete paradigms is Joyce Burland's "Stages of Emotional Responses." Dr. Burland is a clinical psychologist who developed a family education course with the National Alliance for the Mentally Ill (NAMI) to help family members like herself understand and cope with their mentally ill relatives. Part of the grieving process with mental illness is mourning the loss of loved ones who may never return to the persons they were before the onset of the illness; we mourn a lost personality while the person is still living. Joyce Burland's stages of response are summarized in the following chart:

STAGES OF EMOTIONAL RESPONSES[7]

I. Dealing with Catastrophic Events
Crisis/Chaos/Shock
Denial; "normalizing"
Hoping Against Hope

Needs: *Support *Comfort *Empathy for confusion *Help finding resources *Crisis intervention *Prognosis *Empathy for pain . . .

II. Learning to Cope
 Anger/Guilt/Resentment
 Recognition
 Grief

 Needs: *Vent feelings *Keep hope *Education *Self-care *Networking *Skill training *Letting go *Co-op from System . . .

III. Moving into Advocacy
 Understanding
 Acceptance
 Advocacy/Action

 Needs: *Activism *Restoring balance in life *Responsiveness from System . . .

This model outlines three main stages of emotions we may experience in dealing with any traumatic event. It is based on the principle that we may get stuck at one of the stages until we get what we need to move on. By inviting us to consider some of the needs that should be met at each stage, this can become a compassionate model as we apply it to our own and to others' mourning. In meeting the needs of others we honor the covenant to "mourn with those that mourn . . . and comfort those that stand in need of comfort" (Mosiah 18:9). Usually this requires us to show empathy and not impose judgments. By seeking the Spirit to know when and how to help one another at each stage, we can join in the work of the Savior who suits "his mercies according to the conditions of the children of men" (D&C 46:15).

Joyce Burland reminds us that "none of these stages are 'wrong' or 'bad.' They are normal."[8] She also states that they can be cyclical, and that "different family members are often at different places in the cycle, which is why we sometimes have difficulty communicating with each other and agreeing on what to do."[9] She further maintains that the process "is not about expectations. This is a human process that you do *your* way. If you know where you are in it you can be more gentle with yourself. . . . It offers hope to see that we *do* progress through pain and grief to acceptance."[10] And, she maintains, as we disclose our emotions to each other we can "validate our feelings."[11]

I remember painfully my feelings—found in the initial stage of Burland's construct—when I caused the death of a small animal I was trying to raise. I was a ten-year-old, fascinated with the "toy bears" that were in a live display at the science fair at Tooele Central. The Syrian golden hamster had just been introduced into the United States a few years before, much rounder and more Panda-like than some of the current varieties. I had to have one. The expense of owning a pair was unheard of, but somehow I managed to earn and plead my way to a male and female that I impatiently raised until they were old enough to start my business. Frustrated by clumsy attempts to get them to breed, I was finally only sixteen gestation days away from owning my first litter. I marked the calendar. On the morning of the day she was to deliver, I found the bulging mother stiff and prostrate in the sawdust. I was in shock.

Hamsters have long cheek pouches that extend most of the length of their bodies in which they hoard food. When I could find no food in the cage, I was sure she had stored the dog biscuits in her pouches. But the pouches were empty, probably had been for at least a week. I denied to myself what had happened. I tried to normalize the situation: it must have been inferior stock; it wasn't my fault; Mom said pregnancies didn't always work out; the mother hamster just got sick and died. I even hoped against hope that she might be hibernating. I was afraid others would find out. Most of all I felt guilty.

From that mistake I date part of my emotional life. I probably suffered from what Jeffrey Kauffman calls "self-disenfranchised grief."[12] I felt so guilty and chagrined by what I had done that I never allowed myself to grieve openly. It was a long time before I admitted responsibility and forgave myself—and even longer before I wanted another pet. You will not find a more nurturing caregiver for animals than the advocate that I eventually became, but only after another traumatic event involving animals years later.

The day my grandfather and I were killing our New Zealand whites that we had been raising for their meat and pelts, I told grandpa I did not want the "white doe" that had been eating her young. California does are white, too, except for their black ears, nose, feet, and tail. Grandpa did not understand English very well; he simply misunderstood me. I came out of the basement where I had gone to get the pelt frame just in time to see him draining the blood from the rabbit I had worked all summer to get the money to buy. I realized in an instant what had happened and tried to conceal my dismay. He quickly figured it out. None of us must have given Grandpa what he needed because he never moved away from the anger he felt with himself for killing my rabbit.

Even in the face of the solemnity of the death of family members, these childhood stages of emotional responses still seem serious to me, so serious in fact that my mind recycles through them every time I confront another death. I loved my Grandpa Miceli very much for all he did with me and for me through years of growing Roma tomatoes together, raising rabbits and banty chickens who came when he called them, making goat cheese, drying chamomile flowers for tea, and taking long bus rides together to visit my sister at the state hospital. At his casket I told him again that what had happened with the rabbit was not his fault.

His was the first death that I remember in our immediate family. I was a teenager at the time and still afraid of death and being around the dead, I think mainly because of the strangeness of it all. I thought it strange that my friend Julie died suddenly at age thirteen from an aggressive cancer only a few days after she had done a benefit dance for the American Cancer Society. I was one of six teenage pallbearers. It was strange too that they buried her "so primly propped" with a doll in a pink, faux fur casket.[13] In later years I realized what Tennyson must have felt as he marked the three grieving Christmases in *In Memoriam*: "And sadly fell our Christmas-eve." "And calmly fell our Christmas-eve:" "And strangely falls our Christmas-eve."[14] Tennyson spent seventeen years cycling through all the stages of emotional response in writing this poem until he finally spiraled into acceptance at the end of the elegy, believing that his friend Hallam was the forerunner of a higher race who would help us move toward that "one far-off divine event,/ To which the whole creation moves."[15] Nonetheless Tennyson saw strangeness in the mystery of death and mourning.

Grandpa's death was strange and my mother's grieving even stranger. In retrospect I realize that her loud wailing during the funeral was acceptable to southern Europeans, even though some of them thought that response should have been left behind in the old country. Burland helps me realize that Mom had to vent her feelings in order to cope and that this was her way of "letting go." Most of us at the funeral lacked the cultural awareness that Doka pleads for and so did not understand her reaction. Vanderlyn Pine says responses to death across cultures can range from resignation to hysteria.[16] The Relief Society sisters were the only ones who seemed to understand; they embraced her no matter what she did, and they continued to bring food to the house. I think Dad was embarrassed. He comes from British stock, and thus regarded handshaking as a little overt; whereas Mom's Italian family feels offended if you don't hug them and kiss them on the lips coming and going, like the Pacific islanders I lived among for a decade in Hawaii. Many of the local Saints there give aloha-filled hugs and kisses to everyone—including their dead before the casket is closed.

Mom's death was psychologically traumatic for me. Up to that point in my life I had never really faced the fact that someday *I* would actually die. I had felt invincible. Joyce Burland cogently explains my attitude: "Much of our sense of safety and our willingness to take risks in life rests on our belief that serious harm or 'real trouble' will never happen to us. It may strike someone else, but we are 'special' and immune to misfortune. . . . As a psychological defense system, the denial of human vulnerability supports our sense of well-being, and fuels our faith that we can choose the challenges we wish to take in life."[17] Suddenly with Mother's death I felt, in the words of Joyce Burland, "vulnerable" and "terrifyingly mortal" and knew that I no longer had "the mantle of magical protection." I was clearly in Stage I.

Mom's death was the beginning of a series—Dad and two sisters all within fifteen months of each other. We joked that once Mom left she started scheduling everyone else. There was no lightheartedness, however, in my feeling that I had neglected her by being away on a study abroad trip in London for six months just prior to her death. She didn't want my family to go to London, but she promised to wait for us until we got back. We returned to the States on a Monday, visited her on a Tuesday, and she died early Sunday morning. She had kept her word. My childhood guilt returned. Capable of neglecting a helpless animal, maybe I had neglected my own mother. She would never have been neglectful. She was generous not only with her time and this world's goods, but also in the uplifting encouragement she gave all her children. She truly believed in *la familia*.

What brought me into acceptance was seeing her in her temple clothes, clothes she had worn as a worker in the Salt Lake temple, clothes my wife and I had washed and ironed for her burial, as we had done once before in Indiana for two of our Institute students who were killed in an automobile accident. I think it was one of Mom's white hankies, as she called them, that made the difference. She held it dutifully in her left hand. Mother was always dutiful, dutiful and meticulous, in living and in housekeeping. She told me after Neil Armstrong visited the moon that she didn't like the moon as much when she found out it was "just a bunch of dirt." Seeing her with that handkerchief assured me she was still doing her duty in a heavenly mansion, and probably sweeping its porch as well.

Before the viewing I was haunted by remembering the exposé of the funeral industry in Jessica Mitford's *The American Way of Death*[18] and was expecting something grim. But Mom's "memory picture" was therapeutic for me. The mortician had performed a restorative wonder. An unusual communication from Mom occurred as I stood with my brother and sister in front of the metal casket Mom insisted on—for her generation it was a status symbol, though now I think hardwood claims that place. On each side of the casket were those torchères that shine upward indirectly. My brother asked me and my sister if we thought Mom had forgiven us for putting her in a care center for her last few months. No sooner had he finished the question than with uncanny timing the lightbulb on the right exploded, showering us and Mom with fine glass. I turned to my brother and said, "I think you just got your answer."

Dad had such a difficult time accepting mother's death that I began to worry early on about how I would handle his future responses. I was experiencing anticipatory grief. He was stuck for several days in a denial stage. He was sure there had been some mistake, that Mom would wake up and tell us that her pacemaker had revived her. For him denial was a protective response; it gave his mind a chance to get its bearing on losing someone he had never been separated from in fifty-nine years. From the week of the funeral on, his health began to decline. Mom's body had given in to diabetes, Parkinson's, angina, arthritis, and a perpetual state of feeling cold year round. Even with these maladies, her mind never failed. Dad was the reverse. His body remained strong up until the last week, even though he suffered from chronic leukemia for years. He outlived the doctor who had diagnosed it and who had pleaded with him to seek treatment. Dad had an aversion to doctors. He repeatedly said they would kill him if he sought treatment. He lived to be eighty-six.

But when he became forgetful, repetitive, and kept asking me if I was his brother Floyd I began to grieve the loss of a man who had read widely, who could carry on conversations on expansive subjects, and who had always reconciled his knowledge with his faith, a faith that motivated him to serve three successful stake missions. I tried to cope by remembering him the way he used to be. Before he died he became semi-conscious for several days and kept crying out, "Mama, I'm coming . . . it won't be long." The day after I last visited him I received word—just before I had to be in a thorny administrative meeting—that he had died. I went ahead with the meeting, never telling anyone what had happened, but thinking, "There should be more time for this."

Within four months of Dad's passing, my sister contracted Guillain-Barré syndrome, a polyneuritis she probably got from a flu shot, a one-in-fifty-million chance the doctor said. She suffered some paralysis and could not swallow, so we were left with an ethical decision. Palma was sixty-five and had suffered with schizophrenia and some developmental disabilities for most of her life. Her medication pileup over a period of forty-eight years was incredible. We had asked her months before if she wanted machines to keep her alive if she became really sick. Her response was simple. She said, "When Mama died Heavenly Father held her hand. Will he hold my hand too?" When we reassured her, she said, "No, I don't want any machines."

Should we intervene or not? An affirmative answer was the only one that seemed right, so for nine days she was tube fed. She rallied and seemed much improved, but within two months she, too, had joined our parents. I was close to my coping threshold as I drove to the rest home to be with my sister in her final hours. I asked the Lord to please help me deal with this. He responded by telling me it was going to be okay and that Mom would be there to help. I really believe she was. The link was somehow in the eyes: both Mom's and Palma's were velvet brown.

By now I was beginning to feel some tolerance for the system of living wills, mortuaries, obituaries, viewings, and burial fees—until I saw Palma in her casket. The mortician had misunderstood us to say Palma wore her hair back. When we saw her, we barely recognized her: she looked masculine. Was this system failure? We tried rearranging the front locks and then fixing them with my pocket comb. Neither attempt helped. Finally my wife and I found ourselves with electric curling iron, spray bottle, and brush, frantically working minutes before the funeral was to begin. The result was adequate, but not the curly-headed sister we remembered.

Just three months later my other sister was diagnosed with a small skin cancer that supposedly had a high cure rate. Even with treatment it spread over her entire body and she was dead within half a year. Sally had been a widow much of her life and was a phenomenal survivor. She had been very dependent on her husband, had never learned to drive, and was shy. She overcame every impediment with amazing grace. It was as if she went into the "Learning to Cope" stage the week of the funeral, came to recognition, and successfully stayed there. In the blessing my brother gave her the week before she went into a coma, he told her that she could choose what she wanted. She told us privately she wanted to go to be with her beloved Perry, and so she did.

I am still not able to understand this last death, although it was four years ago. It was too sudden, too ill-advised, too soon after the three others, and too close to my wife's losing her mother and then two sisters to cancer. And there were others soon after: aunts Alice and Melba; uncles Jim, Guy, and Jerry. I spoke at six of the twelve funerals. My not being able to resolve Sally's death is not because I lack faith that all my loved ones are in that state of rest Alma speaks of (Alma 40:12). That is a reality for me. I look forward to the Resurrection, when our burdened bodies and spirits will be, to use

Hopkins's image, as "uncumberèd" as a "rainbow footing" on a "meadow down."[19] I think I am not able to let go because I feel I should have done more for her. To bring closure would in a sense be admitting that I didn't do enough and that it is too late. I suppose that is a type of denial. So I keep circling for now, hoping for that spiral.

Joyce Burland believes "'coming to terms' with grief is *hardest* . . . for people who are very capable, who are used to solving problems, who are accustomed to making things happen, who are highly motivated to overcome every obstacle."[20] But, of course, with death we sometimes cannot solve its cause, make it not happen, or hurdle the obstacles it presents, no matter what our abilities are. We cannot *control* physical death; and sometimes we may feel we cannot control grief either. Thus one of the principles of support in the Journey of Hope family education program is that "we acknowledge that there is a higher power to whom we will turn to nurture and strengthen our ability to release control over things we cannot control."[21] For me that "higher power" is our Heavenly Father, the Savior, and the Holy Ghost. When we cast our burden on the Lord, He sends comforters from both sides of the veil to help us with what we need, so that we can "bear one another's burdens, that they may be light" (Mosiah 18:8).

One of those comforters for my wife, Dawn, and me is Joyce Burland. Training with her to teach her inspired family education course saved our emotional lives when we were near despair in working with our mentally ill loved ones. She empowered us with knowledge about these illnesses and taught us to recognize our feelings and seek the help we needed. Those same principles have helped us cope with the many recent deaths of our family members. Familiarity with the concepts of emotional stages gives us a metalanguage to discuss our own grief and to help us recognize the responses to death in those around us in their own individual and cultural circumstances. Initially that is best done by applying Dr. Burland's definition of empathy: "The intimate comprehension of another person's thoughts and feelings, without imposing our own judgement [sic] or expectations."[22] Once we have confirmed another person's feelings, often through reflective listening, then we can make suggestions. It helps to disclose our feelings to those who are grieving because in a sense that disclosure gives them permission to disclose their feelings. It is comforting to know we are not alone, that what we are feeling others have felt. The emotional stages model gives us concepts that we can then discuss together. As we do this we often move into the understanding and advocacy stage.

Understanding the stages of grief can also be gained vicariously through art. Richard Attenborough's popular film *Shadowlands*, for example, is a case study of C. S. Lewis, played by Anthony Hopkins, cycling through all the stages of response after the death of his wife, Joy Gresham, played by Debra Winger. The condoling platitudes Lewis receives from his Oxford colleagues do not give him what he needs and he is stuck in anger. It is not until he and Joy's son, Douglas, disclose their feelings and weep in one another's arms that he is able to let go. "After great pain," Emily Dickinson says, "a formal feeling comes—/ . . . First—Chill—then Stupor—then the letting go."[23] That describes Lewis. After letting go he comes to some acceptance of Joy's death by acknowledging that through loving others we may come "to know we are not alone."[24]

Joy, on the other hand, comes to accept loss more readily. In a scene left out of the Attenborough film, but included in the William Nicholson play and in Norman Stone's BBC film version of the story, Joy is in shock when her first husband deserts her. Unable to get the help she needs from those she knows, she is comforted by a higher power:

> We were living in Westchester County. Bill was working in the city. One day he phoned from his office to say he was losing control of his mind and that he wasn't ever coming home. Bang went the phone down. That was it. I had a small baby. I was alone. I had no idea what to do. I phoned everyone I knew. They hadn't seen Bill. I put the baby to bed, and I waited. He didn't come. I didn't know if he was dead or alive. Round about midnight, I broke down. I never felt so helpless in my life. The baby was upstairs asleep. I was downstairs. I was crying. Then there was someone else in the room. Just for a few seconds, maybe half a minute. But I knew it was a real person. More real than real. So real everything else was like shadows. I said something, I've no idea what. I guess I was just saying, Okay then. Okay.[25]

My wife and I felt a "real person" with us in the Salt Lake Temple a few months after my mother died. Our family had done endowments and sealings for Mom's immediate family but had somehow neglected to get Grandma Miceli sealed to Grandpa Miceli. Temple workers called us to say they were anxious for us to correct the oversight and asked if we could come to the temple that week to do it. Two days later we were in the sealing room with two prospective missionaries and a mother of one of the missionaries that the workers had recruited to assist. As the sealing was being performed everyone in the room felt my mother's presence, even though the witnesses were total strangers to us. Accompanying that presence was the enveloping assurance that all was forgiven, the exploded lightbulb notwithstanding. Since that temple experience my grief over my mother has remained resolved.

Another comforter came to help us cope with anticipatory grief when our second grandson was born three months premature. Preston weighed only one pound fifteen ounces. His hand could almost fit through my daughter's wedding ring. In the intensive care unit we reached between the tubes and wires to give him a blessing. Unsure at first of what was best for Preston at that moment, the direction was suddenly clear: we pleaded for guardian angels to minister to him and watch over him. My wife, Dawn, was at home praying while we were giving the blessing. The same directions came to her. She remembered a promise her mother and father made to each other a few days before her mother died. Eleanor was regretting not being able to stay and help nurture her grandchildren, so LaVarr said that if she would take care of the grandchildren from her side of the veil, he would take care of them on this side. Each morning as we visited Preston in the hospital, we wondered who Eleanor would send that day to help him. Today Preston is an active, healthy three-year-old. His grandmother had made our responses to loss unnecessary.

Understanding the stages of emotional responses in an individual cultural context is ultimately for me a call to service, service to ourselves and then to others. This is the pattern I see invited over and over again in the Book of Mormon—restore balance in your own life and then reach out generously to others. It is part of the advocacy of Stage III. It is not an easy journey, but one that I trust will lift us on a celestial spiral out of the burdens of our grief.

NOTES

1. See Elisabeth Kübler-Ross, *On Death and Dying* (New York: Macmillan Publishing Co., 1969).
2. *Relief Society Handbook* (Salt Lake City: The Church of Jesus Christ of Latter-day Saints, 1988), p. 38.
3. Andrew Weil, *Spontaneous Healing* (New York: Alfred A. Knopf, 1995), p. 83.
4. Kenneth J. Doka in *Living with Grief: Who We Are, How We Grieve*, ed. Kenneth J. Doka and Joyce D. Davidson (Washington, D.C.: Hospice Foundation of America, 1998), p. 1.
5. Ibid.
6. Ibid., p. 2.
7. Joyce Burland, *NAMI Family-to-Family Education Program Teaching Manual*, 2d edition (Arlington: National Alliance for the Mentally Ill, 1998): 1.g., used by permission.
8. Ibid. 1.6.
9. Ibid.
10. Ibid.
11. Ibid.
12. Jeffrey Kauffman, "Intrapsychic Dimensions of Disenfranchised Grief," in *Disenfranchised Grief*, ed. Kenneth J. Doka (Lexington, MA: Lexington Books, 1989), pp. 25–32.
13. John Crowe Ransom, "Bells for John Whiteside's Daughter," in *John Crowe Ransom Selected Poems* (New York: Alfred A. Knopf, 1969), p. 7.
14. Alfred, Lord Tennyson, *In Memoriam*, 30.4; 78.4; 105.4, as found in *In Memoriam: An Authoritative Text, Backgrounds and Sources, Criticism*, ed. Robert H. Ross (New York: W.W. Norton & Company, 1973).
15. Ibid., Epilogue 143.
16. See Vanderlyn Pine, "Death, Loss, and Disenfranchised Grief," in *Disenfranchised Grief* (1989), pp. 13–23.
17. Burland (1998): 7.2–7.3.
18. See Jessica Mitford, *The American Way of Death*, (New York: Simon & Schuster, 1963).
19. Gerard Manley Hopkins, "The Caged Skylark," in *Poems and Prose of*

Gerard Manley Hopkins, sel. W. H. Gardner (Baltimore: Penguin Books, 1953), p. 32.

20. Burland (1998): 9.10.

21. "Principles of Support," no. 10, *Journey of Hope: A Support and Family Education Program Facilitator's Manual* (Baton Rouge: Louisiana Alliance for the Mentally Ill, 1992): 11-3.

22. Burland (1998): 7.e.

23. Emily Dickinson, *The Complete Poems of Emily Dickinson*, ed. Thomas H. Johnson (Boston: Little, Brown and Company, 1976), p. 162.

24. Richard Attenborough, *Shadowlands*, Spelling Films International, 1993.

25. William Nicholson, *Shadowlands* (New York: Plume, 1991), pp. 36–37.

THESE ARE THE THINGS WE KNOW
by Nicea Stimpson Gedicks

It was Thursday, November 13, 1997, only three months to the day since Alex had boarded a plane in Salt Lake City bound for his first college adventure. It was clear outside and cool, just the kind of November day we've come to love in Orem, Utah. Our oldest daughter, Annie, almost eighteen, was a senior at Orem High School. Abby, our ninth grader, was fifteen, and our youngest daughter, Amanda, was almost eleven. My husband, Fred, a law professor at Brigham Young University, had left two days earlier to present a paper at an academic conference in Italy and would be gone for a week. Alex, our oldest child and only son, was a freshman on a full-tuition ROTC scholarship at Wake Forest University. He had turned nineteen during the semester and had received his mission call to serve in the Connecticut Hartford Mission. He was to enter the Missionary Training Center on New Year's Eve.

On a trip to Salt Lake City three of my friends and I had spoken of our sons and their missions. One friend had a son already serving in Boston, the other two friends had younger boys who would be making missionary decisions in a few years. As the sometimes fretting mom I can be, I was concerned that Alex hadn't formally accepted his mission call after three weeks. Had he decided college was too

---

Nicea Stimpson Gedicks *lives in Orem, Utah, with her husband, Fred, and three daughters. She loves to read and participate in book clubs, and spends much of her time volunteering in her children's schools. Nicea is currently homemaking leader in her ward, which she considers a delightful break.*

much fun to leave for two years? Was he going to change his mind?

My fears were squelched when I arrived home and got the mail. There was Alex's letter to the Brethren, written in his familiar left-handed scrawl, short, sweet, and sincere, accepting his call to serve the Lord in Connecticut. He was doing the will of the Lord because he wanted to. It was with a full heart of love, gratitude, and respect that I laid the envelope on our kitchen table. I would give it to Bishop Snow that evening for his signature, then he would mail it to the missionary committee the next day. This would be good news to give Fred when he called in a day or so.

I felt giddy with peace as I arranged on the hearth a Christmas pine tree I had purchased that day. I wanted to create a warm and welcome Christmas atmosphere for Alex's return from college and his departure to the mission field. The girls would come home from school soon, there was dinner to prepare. All was right in my world. I unpacked my purchases, basking in the warm glow of contentment. Life seemed utterly and perfectly good at that moment, one of those times you'd like to freeze in place forever.

Forty minutes later the phone rang. It was Dr. Earl Schwartz, with a foreshadowing of news that would change my life forever. He told me he was worried about Alex, who had checked into the student health center that morning with a sore throat and had just been transported by ambulance to the emergency room at Baptist Hospital in downtown Winston-Salem. I asked the doctor how serious Alex was. His reply was direct and stern: "Mrs. Gedicks, I'm worried about your son." I remember wondering to myself, What exactly does this mean? Severe illness? Complications that might have lasting side effects? Disability? Brain damage? Dr. Schwartz told me he suspected meningitis or Rocky Mountain spotted fever, but at that point Alex still had none of the symptoms—no stiff neck, no headache, no rash, and negative blood tests for the bacteria they were looking for. The staff at the health center had been treating him for a viral sore throat all day. His temperature was 102.5 when he was admitted, and he had been given fluids. They had also given him Tylenol and an anti-nausea medication that made him drowsy, so he had slept most of the day.

What was the right question for me to ask next, the one that would tell me what was really going on? "Do I need to be there?" I expected a no-he's-going-to-be-fine response. What Dr. Schwartz said next made my heart sink. "Mrs. Gedicks, you need to get here as soon as you possibly can." I still never thought Alex was going to die; nobody dies from a cold. But a sickening feeling thudded on my insides, telling me that the urgency of the situation was more real than I was admitting.

Amanda came home from school just then and heard the end of my conversation with Dr. Schwartz. I explained the situation and led her to the family room sofa, where I wrapped my arms around her shoulders and prayed with her, asking Heavenly Father to "please bless Alex to get better." I put in the part about letting His will be done. Amanda felt better after that. She is so trusting in her worried sort of way, but I couldn't put aside the feeling that the Lord's will was going to be done, and I wasn't going to like it. Unaware of the mounting dread I was feeling, Amanda asked if she could go to a friend's house to play.

My first impulse after the phone conversation with Dr. Schwartz was to make plane reservations immediately, but I knew it would be hours at best before I could get to Alex. I was impatient with the thought of the tediously slow motions of making reservations and physically boarding a plane. If I could just be there now. If the clock would just stop until I arrived. I felt a helpless feeling, like being carried along in a current I couldn't control. But it never felt bleak, or black, just out of my hands.

Plane reservations would have to wait: Alex needed a priesthood blessing. I remembered a telephone number I'd been given back in September when I had visited Alex at school, the number of Ed Allen, the counselor in Alex's Winston-Salem bishopric who had taken an interest in Alex when he saw his religious affiliation listed on the registrar's rolls at Wake Forest. Ed is a math professor on campus. I had written his number on an index card and placed it in my scriptures where it had remained unnoticed for the last two months until it fell into my lap during Sunday School just five days earlier. I called Ed, asking him if he could arrange to give Alex a blessing. Ed knew two LDS medical students at Wake Forest who might be at the hospital.

I still never thought Alex would die. At worst I thought I might spend several weeks in the hospital by his bed, supporting and loving him back to health. One of his best friends had beat spinal meningitis just three months earlier, though his recovery had been long. I packed my suitcase for the trip with clothes I'd be comfortable in during the long hours of hospital vigilance I anticipated. I had packed a dress for church, but realized I probably wouldn't be going to church if Alex were this ill, so I replaced it with another pair of pants and a sweater. Ironically, I would have to purchase a dress for memorial services four days later.

I knew even a short illness would annoy Alex, make him impatient with mundane things like eating and sleeping. He'd be angry if his final exams or his entrance into the mission field were delayed. He had a plan, and so far the plan had run like clockwork. Shortly before 5:00 P.M. Ed Allen called back from Winston-Salem. The medical students had given Alex a blessing, feeling prompted to bless him to recover. I was relieved to hear those words, and Ed's voice was calm. But I believe we know in our souls truths that our minds are slow to grasp, and my mind simply would not acknowledge the gut feeling of finality that had already planted itself inside me. It was there like a huge, black, lifeless mass, plain as day. I consciously ignored it as if my doing so would make it disappear.

For the next four hours I was confused by conflicting feelings. I acted on faith as I had done countless other times in my life, but this time seemed different. Deeper down was the feeling that I was being swept along in that current that was bigger and stronger than myself, and there was nothing I could do about it. The feeling seemed neither good nor bad, just there.

With the help of my friend Jane Clark I completed preparations for my trip to North Carolina. Bishop Snow had come to the house when I called him after speaking to Ed Allen. He had made travel arrangements by cellular phone on his way. It was too late to catch the 5:30 flight; the next one out was at 8:30. Fred's mother, "Nana," would take care of the girls and his dad, "Papa," would drive me to the airport.

It's remarkable how guided I was even before I heard the dreadful news. Answers came almost before questions. I was able to make decisions that ordinarily might have caused me hours of agonizing thought. Later I would recognize the Comforter for what it was, but at the time it seemed like I was being pulled through the necessary motions.

Annie came home from her after-school activities. I briefed her on Alex's situation, and she hugged me, compassionate as always. I told her about the blessing Alex had received and she seemed to relax, but kept her feelings inside as she tends to do. I told her we'd talk when she got back from her next commitment, but she returned after I had to leave for the airport and our talk never happened. Abby had gone straight from school to the dance studio. I hadn't seen her since that morning, when she ran out the door to the bus, toast in one hand, a change of clothes in the other, and a backpack heavier than she is over her shoulder. She knew nothing of what had transpired that afternoon, and burst into tears in my arms when she heard the news.

It was awful to leave the girls in such an unsettled state. With Fred in Italy at the conference, Alex lying ill on the other side of the continent, and my daughters staying behind in Utah, I felt the full burden of responsibility for holding everyone and everything together. While I had known about Alex's condition for nearly three hours by now, Fred knew nothing. Attempts to reach him at the number he'd left on his itinerary were futile. Fred's sister Robin would continue the effort.

At about 7:00 P.M. Papa and I left for the airport. I was surprisingly calm on the surface, and the inner turmoil had subsided noticeably. Bishop Snow had loaned me a cellular telephone to use on my trip. Nana called me a couple of times on it before we arrived at the airport. The third time she called she gave me a message off our home answering machine from a Dr. Jerry Blaine at Baptist Hospital. Nana was crying. I asked her if the message sounded serious. She didn't know.

We rounded the corner to the curbside check-in at Salt Lake International Airport. Papa stopped his truck and as he lifted my suitcase from the back, I placed the call to Dr. Blaine. "This is Gerry Blaine," a woman's voice answered. Because I had spoken earlier with Dr. Schwartz I was surprised to hear the voice of a woman, perhaps my mind's way of stalling for time. If I didn't focus on the impending reality, maybe it wouldn't materialize.

"Is this *Dr.* Jerry Blaine?" I asked, picturing in my mind's eye a male with a different spelling. If I had the wrong doctor and if there were bad news, then the news wouldn't be for me. "Yes," she said. "This is Nicea Gedicks, Alex Gedicks's mother." There was a pause, then Dr. Blaine asked, "Is this *Alexander* Gedicks's mother?" My mind raced. Why had she paused and been so careful to clarify? "Yes," I said. And then the quiet voice of the doctor who seemed as far away as the other side of the world said these dreaded words: "Mrs. Gedicks, I'm sorry to have to tell you this over the telephone, but your son didn't make it."

Never in a million years did I think I would ever hear something like this. Such things didn't happen to me. I could always get out of the worst situations through prayer, through repentance, through hard work. There is always a way out. It simply could not be. I remember saying over and over again, "I can't believe this. I can't believe this."

But I knew. And I knew there was nothing I could do. I could not make him better or bring him back. Even as my mind raced around frantically, seeking a remedy, a solution, a compromise, a miracle, my heart knew as surely as anything I've ever known in my life that this was reality, the way it was. I couldn't fix it or change it. I couldn't talk it over or make a deal. I was thinking that when I awoke tomorrow it would be just as real as it was at that moment. A nap wouldn't ease it or a good night's sleep erase it. No glue would repair it, nor medicine cure it. I couldn't buy a new one or mend or sew the old one. It was final.

My mind finally caught up to my heart, and I knew at that moment what was required of me: submission, complete and unquestioning submission to my Father's will. He required it, and I, who always planned ahead, orchestrated, and liked to control the happenings in my life, needed to give it. I needed to rely on the Lord.

I accepted the reality. The little boy I'd hugged and kissed and chased and laughed with, the young boy I'd watched play soccer and baseball and swim in relays, the teenager who'd become the editor of his high school newspaper, gone to Boys State and become the English Sterling Scholar at Orem High, the young man who'd taken his priesthood responsibilities seriously and who had won scholarships to BYU and Wake Forest, this vibrant, healthy nineteen-year-old who had worked out at the gym and was conscious of his health (except for not getting enough sleep), who prayed and studied the scriptures, who liked camping, ultimate Frisbee, and girls as much as he liked good food, who had made me laugh and cry all in the same day—*my boy* was dead.

I told Papa the awful news, and he put his arms around me. Though an airport is among the noisiest places on the planet, I could hear no sounds. I was aware of movement, cars driving by, an airport official watching me, people walking. Yet I felt as if I were suspended in still water, as if I were in an aquarium without the pump. The muffled and buffered feelings were comforting. I felt warm and protected. I began to function again on spiritual autopilot. That sensation I'd felt at home of being carried along by a gentle force greater than myself suddenly had a name: the Comforter. I've heard people say that the feeling is tangible. It is.

Dr. Blaine said she understood that I was on my way to North Carolina, and advised that I shouldn't travel alone. She asked if there was anyone who could come with me. Papa unhesitatingly agreed to come, with only the clothes on his back. The plane was leaving in less than half an hour.

Glenda Stout, a Delta employee standing just inside the entrance to the airport, greeted me as I walked through the doors red-eyed and shocked. I explained my situation to her and she jumped into action. Within minutes she had changed our flight to a later one, which eliminated a leg of the trip that would have taken us through Denver. The new flight arrived in Winston-Salem at the same time as the prior flight, but allowed us four hours of extra time on the ground to make phone calls. I remember thinking I would never survive an all-nighter with no sleep and a full day of who-knew-what in North Carolina. But I never felt tired, never even got the headache that I always get when I lack sleep. The Comforter had descended, and I was blanketed with warm assurances as I was ushered through these uncharted waters.

I called Bishop Snow from the ticket counter to tell him of our changed plans and asked him to break the news to Annie and the others. I wish I could have done it myself, but I didn't want them to hear it over the telephone as I had. It would be a hard time for everyone. Glenda ushered us to a room upstairs and provided us with tissues, water, and a telephone. She was an angel, staying with us until well after her shift had ended. An hour later, Paul Clark, a member of our bishopric, was with us in the airport. On his way home from Logan he had received a call that we were at the airport and came straight over.

I remember wiping tears from my eyes as I said to Paul, "We believe that Alex's spirit is in the spirit world, right? That he is actively engaged in a good work and is happy there? And we believe that his body will be reunited with his spirit in the Resurrection and that we'll be with him again? These are the things we believe, right?" I sort of blurted this out, and Paul's reply, firm and resolute, was like warm hands around my heart: "Nicea, these are the things we *know*." This was precisely the moment at which I knew what my further course should be. It felt like a remembering of things I'd learned long, long ago, perhaps before I ever came here. "The Comforter, which is the Holy Ghost, whom the Father will send in my name . . . shall . . . bring all things to your remembrance, whatsoever I have said unto you" (John 14:26).

There were no specific words—like there would be later at Wake Forest—but rather a sure direction, in spite of my disbelief of the news of Alex's death. I knew I had to live the testimony I had always professed to have and which had never been seriously challenged before. I needed to act as I believed. To carry on in agony would suggest that I didn't truly believe the plan of salvation. To hold my head up and give strength to those around me would show my Heavenly Father that I trusted what I'd learned all my life growing up in the Church: death is just a natural part of life, a doorway into our third estate, and Alex had moved through that door. Someone would later quote to me, "Pain is inevitable but misery is optional." I would feel the pain but I would refuse to be miserable. The plan of salvation working in my life wasn't just a nice story any more. It lived. I knew I'd still be crying, but I felt calm and assured, that all was as it should be.

Fred had finally been reached by Bishop Snow and I had spoken with him briefly by phone from the airport before our plane took off at midnight. Papa and I arrived in Winston-Salem at about 9:30 A.M. Friday and were met by Ed Allen, Sherrie Ritchie, and Christine Rathburn from Alex's Winston-Salem Ward, plus Lieutenant Colonel Buz Moser in full dress uniform, representing Wake Forest University and the ROTC. I was deeply touched by their presence. They remained graciously at our disposal for the next four days until we returned to Utah.

Ed drove us to the Graylyn Mansion on campus where we would be staying, then chauffeured us to the hospital where we were met by Chaplain Mark Jensen, who had arranged for me to talk with all the doctors who had treated Alex. We sat around a large conference table, and each took a turn recounting for me the last twelve hours of Alex's life and the part they had played in it. I took notes, knowing that I would need to fill Fred in when he arrived that night, and wanting to get the story entirely straight for our daughters and Alex's many friends who would be waiting for us when we returned.

I was moved by their humility and love. The doctors had done all that they could. Somehow Alex had contracted a meningococcus infection from the same bacteria that causes pneumonia, meningitis, and sore throats—a common bacteria carried by up to thirty percent of the American population at any given time. The bacteria had entered Alex's bloodstream and attacked his organs, causing a rapidly cascading effect of organ failures. The last doctor to speak told of doing CPR on Alex for forty-five minutes after his heart stopped beating, hoping and praying for a miracle for such a vibrant, well-loved young man. At the end of the session, this doctor, a big man with white hair, rose from the table and walked toward me, tears streaming down his cheeks. He bent down and hugged me and told me how sorry he was. He too had a nineteen-year-old son living away from home at college.

Fred arrived that night from Italy, physically and emotionally exhausted. We went straight to bed, and the next morning met again briefly with Chaplain Jensen and two of the doctors. It was excruciating for me to watch Fred. He had learned by telephone with no previous warning of the death of his only son. He'd been alone on the nineteen-hour flight from Italy. He was overwhelmed. When he broke down it was almost more than I could bear. But I had begun to notice how tangible the unseen hands were that lifted me. I began to feel the prayers of others. I was witnessing the gospel of Jesus Christ in its purest form: mourning with those that mourn and bearing one another's burdens. It doesn't get more basic than that. People, regardless of their religious affiliation, were surrounding us with love.

Alex's classmates and friends from Wake Forest met with us at the ROTC building. I will never forget the spirit of the kids who sat with us and swapped stories about Alex. Some were so funny we laughed until we cried a different kind of tear. One boy came to us after the meeting and said, "I just want you to know that Alex was a man of God." They all had known about his plans to leave school at the end of the semester to become a missionary. Because of them we became better acquainted with Alex, and so did they. We still correspond with some of these spirited young people.

At Alex's dorm another group of students was assembled. We spoke briefly to them, then went into his room to pack up his belongings. I thought it would be difficult, but what I saw when I began opening drawers was yet another blessing for a mother: they were full of clean, folded clothes. His laundry basket had only one or two items in it. My son had actually learned to take care of himself! It struck me as ironic that his bedroom at home was still littered with debris from nineteen years of collections but his dorm room was in order.

The parents of Alex's roommate offered to finish the packing while we visited with the students assembled outside the door. We learned that Alex was close to getting an ultimate Frisbee team chartered on campus, and that he was a champion at "conquering the table" in his spare time. This meant climbing atop a small end table in the commons room and, without touching the floor with any body part, working oneself all the way underneath the table and back onto the top again. He could climb walls with the best of them, and had wallpapered the lounge walls and ceiling with flyers from campus bulletin boards, only to be told to take them down because they presented a fire hazard. Undaunted, he laid out a golf course one night at 3:00 A.M. in the formal parlor. "We took many divots from the carpet and walls," his journal records, "and replaced some of them."

Back in the hotel room I had just straightened the bedspread on my side of the bed when a thought came into my head that caused me to stand straight up. It was as if words just like those on this page were being typed, letter by letter, across the front of my brain: "Take this good feeling back to Utah." It was a powerful, clear, unmistakable directive to me, one I could not ignore. I knew that there were some pretty sad kids in Orem—our girls and Alex's friends, not to mention our own friends and relatives. They had not had the healing opportunities Fred and I had experienced in North Carolina. We needed to share the warmth with them. I suggested to Fred that we call Stuart, one of Alex's best friends, and ask him to assemble as many kids as would like to participate in a gathering at our house on Monday evening to share the details of Alex's death.

Fred and I were unable to see Alex's body until Saturday night. I was uncomfortable that the finality might be more than I could handle or that he would look completely different. My relief was exquisite when I walked into the room and saw him, dressed in a hospital gown but otherwise looking exactly as he should have. We walked directly over to him and tears flooded my eyes and flowed down my cheeks. I touched his face and laughed at myself when he didn't flinch as I had been conditioned by him to expect over the last few years. I couldn't help myself from bending over and placing my cheek next to his. His cheek was cold, but I imagined that he had just come in from one of his winter outings at home, and it felt as natural as that. I stroked his short, curly brown hair and I felt his hands. It was so wonderful to be close to him without his drawing back. It was as right as anything could be.

We walked a few feet away, just across the room, and sat and admired our stripling warrior. My heart couldn't contain the pride. He was big and handsome and righteous. I was his mother, and he was sealed to us. I knew I could endure the time, however long, until we were reunited. At that moment, eternity seemed so close. I believe that when we look back at our time on earth we will see how incredibly short it was, like years and years passing as a single day. We knew when it was time to leave the mortuary. There was no desire to linger longer, though I could have gone on forever holding Alex in my arms. Another unseen hand had led us through an experience with distressing possibilities. Instead we were lifted, taught, and comforted.

The Spirit was strong in Alex's Winston-Salem ward the next day. The bishopric and Alex's home teacher spoke of the Atonement and the Resurrection of Jesus Christ. I know that hearts were touched. Following the service, Jeff Broberg, the young elders' quorum president, took us into a small classroom and told us what had been said in the blessing given to Alex by the two LDS medical students in the emergency room. Again the Spirit was tangible. Jeff said that when the students arrived at Alex's bedside he had been in and out of consciousness. The doctors had ordered him intubated to help with his breathing, but had not yet started the procedure. The students asked Alex if he would like his blessing now or after the intubation, and he, conscious now of their presence, said, "Now." The privacy curtain was drawn and one of the elders pronounced the blessing. He told Alex that this was not a random event, that the Lord was with him and in control, and that he would still be able to serve his mission. At that point they both saw Alex visibly relax. The doctors returned and the tube was inserted down Alex's throat. Minutes later he was rushed to the ICU, and fifteen minutes after that his heart pumped its last.

Tears streamed down Jeff's cheeks and ours. For a moment no one could speak as we absorbed the magnitude of the plan we were all a part of, and as we felt the Savior's love for each of us. I felt the personal nature of His sacrifice and felt Him very near. Alex had entered into eternity, and we knew it. He had been embraced by his elder brother Jesus Christ, "the keeper of the gate . . . and he employeth no servant there" (2 Nephi 9:41). How good he must feel. Fred has often said that Alex's death is not a tragedy. Alex had prepared himself for a mission and had been worthy to be ordained an elder. He had signed and accepted his mission call, charted his course on a righteous path.

Sometimes Fred and I shake our heads in disbelief. How did Alex end up at Wake Forest University in the first place? We believe his acceptance there was one of many events put in place to prepare us for his death. He had written Wake Forest as one of his choices when he applied for an early consideration ROTC scholarship. In the fall of Alex's senior year of high school, he was awarded the scholarship to attend BYU, but not one to attend Wake Forest or his third choice, Duke University.

Coupled with the academic scholarship that he would be awarded soon and Fred's faculty tuition benefit, Alex could have gone to BYU and lived in the dorms for nothing, money in his pocket. We told him we'd pretend that we lived far away, and promised not to call him every day. But having lived in Orem since he was twelve, with BYU in his back yard, Alex had wanted to expand his horizons. He was disappointed that he had not been awarded a scholarship to Wake Forest or Duke, knowing that we could not afford to send him there without one.

But Alex's ROTC scholarship application had been recycled through the regular scholarship consideration process. In mid-March, long after all the college application deadlines, Alex was notified he had been awarded the ROTC's biggest scholarship to attend Wake Forest. It would provide for all of his tuition and fees, books, plus a spending allowance for four years, and the university would throw in room and board as an added incentive. They were even willing to defer everything while he served a two-year mission for the Church. Just one problem—in the absence of a scholarship, he hadn't *applied* to Wake Forest. The ROTC officials were so sure Alex was the type of student who would be an asset to both Wake Forest and the military that they personally delivered his application to the admissions committee even though the deadline was long past. Within a few days he was admitted.

We had all summer with Alex and had enjoyed a trip to Disneyland, a family reunion in San Francisco, and three days on the beach, but it seemed the time for his departure to school arrived too quickly. Alex was ready to move on but none of us was really ready to have him go. I couldn't believe where we were in our lives. I still felt like a little girl in some ways, yet here I was sending my boy off to college. He had worked hard. He deserved it. He wanted it, and so did we.

When we said good-bye at the airport he bent over and gave me a hug I will cherish forever. I kissed his cheek and told him how much I loved him. There was so much more I wanted to say, but I knew this was already hard enough for him and us, so I held back. He hugged his dad, who told him he loved him and how proud he was of him. Alex would later quote Fred in an E-mail to a friend, telling how much it meant to hear his dad say, "I'm proud of you, Son, so proud."

Alex turned and walked toward the gate, backpack over his shoulder and ticket in hand. He was so handsome in his blue shirt, his pants that bagged a little at the ankles, and his hiking boots. My heart ran over. Would he ever know how much I loved him and how I would miss him? We watched until his plane was out of sight. Already there was a hollow spot in our lives. Neither of us said much over lunch. It seemed abnormal to feel such gut-wrenching loneliness already. Did other parents feel this way?

My friend Nancy Anderson asked me the following day how we were doing. I told her that putting Alex on the plane was the hardest thing I had done in his lifetime. She told me about some friends of hers who had recently put their son in the MTC. They had trouble controlling their emotions, too, so they went for a walk and decided to keep walking until they stopped crying. Nancy said they just kept circling the block. I am still circling my block.

Alex sensed that his leaving for college signalled a momentous change. "I love all my friends, I don't want to leave them," he E-mailed one friend. "What's going to happen in three years? Are they all going to be strong in the Church still? Will someone be dead? Married? There are some people I said good-bye to that I will never see again." Since his death these letters have become all the more poignant. This excerpt from the one he wrote to his friend Stuart is prescient:

> I'm writing you this letter as a kind of farewell memento. I would like you to know that I have enjoyed to the greatest degree getting to know you this year. I consider you one of my best and closest friends and I would like to thank you for this friendship. We have had some incredible times, ya think? The trip to DC, getting prom dates, chess, Sterling Scholars, Model UN, girls. I will remember and cherish the times always.
>
> But this needs to be said, and I think it is said well in Alma 17:2. Our friendship is all for naught if either of us falls away. I wholly expect to be worthy to go on my mission in December, and I expect you to be, too, so I can "rejoice exceedingly" to see my

brethren, and adding to my joy, see that they are still my "brethren in the Lord."

This may be a farewell letter, but make no mistake, it is merely temporary. Don't think you're rid of me, Stu, just because I'm clear across the continent. I'll be back! And I *will* see you again. You're not going to get rid of me that easily. We will meet again (Alma 17:13).

So have fun at BYU. Get good grades. And let me just say that I love you. I know that God lives. I believe in Jesus Christ and the Atonement. I have a testimony of prayer and of the scriptures, and I know that if you read and pray daily and nightly, you will have a change of heart. You will no longer have a desire to do evil (Alma 19:33), and you will only seek things good and righteous. You will seek to find Christ in all things.

Keep the faith.
Until we meet again,
Alex

Both Fred and I got to visit Alex at Wake Forest. I had intended to go with him to help him get settled, but the death of my sister the week he left precluded that. I went two weeks later and saw how completely happy he was. I met his friends, attended his ward, and fell in love with the campus. He showed me his mailbox and Wait Chapel, where his own memorial service would be held some two months later. We ate lunch in "the Pit" and I took pictures of him in his room. I didn't want to leave him, and one night after dropping him at his dorm, I circled it half a dozen times looking up at his window as I passed, hoping to get one more glimpse of him.

Fred visited in October and felt the same way, that Wake Forest was where Alex was meant to go, where he truly belonged. Following his death we would read this excerpt from his journal, written on his first day on campus: "I *own* this place. This is not Wake Forest University, it's Alexander University. I'm going to school everybody. Everyone's going to Alexander school, and they all belong to me. I'm really pumped to get going." It is a great comfort knowing that Alex died at a time when he was as happy as he had ever been in his life.

I have always thought that the worst thing that could happen to me was to lose one of my children. In fact, several years ago, when

Alex was beginning junior high school, I found a series of greeting cards made for adolescents and teenagers. One that I saved still makes me laugh and cry:

What a Parent *Says:*	What a Parent *Means:*
"You're going out without a jacket?"	"If you go out without a jacket, you might catch cold and die and I'll miss you."
"No, you can't stay out late."	"If you stay out late, you won't get enough sleep, and you'll get sick and die and I'll miss you."
"Do your homework."	"If you don't do your homework, you'll grow up to be a bum, get sick and die and I'll miss you."
"I love you."	"I love you." (And I really mean that!)

It still seems unbelievable that the unthinkable happened in my life. When I look at the clinical description of Alex's last hours, I still wonder that a healthy young man in perfect shape can die of a bacterial infection in the 1990s. Maybe he didn't get enough sleep—he had a tendency to pack more into a day than there was physically room for. Maybe he wasn't eating his vegetables—he didn't have time to deal with the mundane. Did he miss washing his hands one too many times before dinner? How did he really catch the bacterial infection that overpowered his organs and caused them all to fail in less than twelve hours? I don't know. But he got sick, and he died, and I miss him.

Some days the lump in my throat threatens to choke me. Reflexively I still reach for the phone when questions come up I'd like to ask him. When did you know you were seriously ill, Alex? Were you ever frightened? Did you know at any time on that November day that you were going to die? Were you given a choice? What did you think of the tributes paid you by your friends at your Wake Forest memorial service? What did you think of your funeral? Is there anything you'd like to say to any of us, your sisters, your dad and me? How about to your friends Marc, Audrey, Stuart, Woolley? Brittany and Beth? Willard, Rob, Tyler, Justin, Nate? Ryan Kellems? The others? Can you believe that Josh is baptized? That Pete is serving in Aunt Shawn's ward in California? What about all of this construction on 800 North?

Elder Neal A. Maxwell spoke in our ward Relief Society the Sunday before Christmas, about six weeks after Alex's death. He spoke on our trials and the Savior's love for us. He said, "If you remember nothing else from my talk today, I want you to remember these four words: It is all right."

And it is.

Chapter Three

THE DEATH OF OUR DAUGHTER: UNEXPECTED APPRENTICESHIP

by Richard H. Cracroft

Jennifer Cracroft Lewis (1968-1994) died suddenly on Wednesday afternoon, January 26, 1994. She was twenty-five years and five months old. She was the wife of Thomas D. Lewis and the only daughter of Janice Alger and Richard Holton Cracroft.

Those stark sentences, supposed to say it all, don't even get close. Any announcement of the death of our beloved daughter should ever after be accompanied by mournful music, eloquent eulogies, and five minutes of silence from San Francisco to Miami and from Zürich to Hong Kong. Any mention of the loss of Jenn should trigger dumbfounded amazement by all men and women everywhere that her parents and her husband have somehow survived. So world-stopping was Jennifer's death that it took a few days for Janice and me to recover from the insulting ignorance of the world—that the ten o'clock news continued to report uneventful eventualities, that school was still held, that unfeeling dogs barked at passersby, that home teachers still waited until the last day of the month to bless their assigned families, with nary a mention by anyone of the most important loss of our generation.

Our experience with the death of our dear girl is this: We have

---

Richard H. Cracroft *lives in Provo with his wife, Janice. They are the parents of three children: Richard, Jeffrey, and Jennifer. Richard is a professor of English at BYU and director of the Center for the Study of Christian Values in Literature. Currently a bishop, he has served as a stake president and president of the Switzerland Zürich Mission.*

been—and continue to be—shattered, grief-stricken, and sorely diminished by her loss. To our muted joy, however, her death has not left us unconsolable. In ways we had not thought possible, Jenn's passing has somehow tested our mettle and tried our faith on the mortal anvil of adversity, making us more malleable and chastened. We have felt our trust in God magnified and our faith reaffirmed. We feel certain and accepting of His purposes, whether or not we understand those purposes. In His mercy, our Father has marked our paths, chastened our human pride, and disclosed our foolish misunderstandings. En route, He has granted us intimations of immortality, firmed our spiritual resolves, and clarified our future course. Thank God.

So Janice and I continue our mortal pilgrimage without our Jennifer, whom we had projected as the loving and enthusiastic traditionalist, historian, cheerleader, and mucilage which would hold our family together; she was the embodiment and exemplar and teacher of our faith, and we counted on her to be the friend and comforter of our old age, as she has been the joy of our youth and middle years. The loss lingers, the hope prevails. And, peculiar dual-beings that we are, we stand at the juncture of the eternal and worldly, still torn both ways. Impatient with the furious hubbub of mortal life, we await the inevitable and glorious reunion of body and spirit. We long for that day when, as Isaiah proclaims, our God and his Christ "will swallow up death in victory; and . . . will wipe away tears from off all faces"(25:8).

Our profound experience in our daughter's death is an intensely private thing, stored up in our souls. We share some of our responses to our loss in hopes that our experience may be a type and shadow of others' grief. We take this opportunity to testify to our fellow grievers (and who is not such?) some of what we have learned en route to finding, as we most assuredly have, heavenly solace amidst mortal loss.

Jenn's Death

Here is how the drama of our daughter's death unfolded for us: disbelief, denial, the collapse of every foundation, and the human rush to place blame somewhere. All of these emotions overwhelmed us a few moments after 7:00 P.M. on that late January evening in 1994 when we learned by telephone from my sister Helen, as we were about to dine at the Salt Lake City home of Swiss-Austrian missionary friends, the news that Tom and our sons had been trying to convey to us since about 3:00 P.M.: Our daughter, Jennifer Cracroft Lewis, was dead of a seizure-induced brain aneurism.

The devastating blow fell without warning. We had been with Jennifer and Tom the evening before. Driving home from Logan, where I had addressed the LDS Institute of Religion at Utah State University, Janice and I had dropped off my sister and her husband at their Bountiful home. We debated briefly whether to drive on home or drop in on Jenn and Tom, who also lived in Bountiful. Although we had just had dinner with them on the previous Saturday and were scheduled to see them later that week, we decided to drop in on them anyway—a decision for which we will always be grateful. Jennifer was glad we stopped by. While waiting for Tom to come home from school at Weber State, we chatted about odds and ends. I watched the televised State of the Union Address while Janice and Jennifer went to the Laundromat and enjoyed a housewife-to-housewife exchange which remains forever fixed in Janice's soul. Folding clothes and chatting, Jenn told her mother, "I feel so domestic, so married (they had just celebrated their first anniversary the previous weekend)—and so happy." Her eyes and face affirmed.

When it was time to depart, the four of us hugged and kissed our good-byes, and, thank the Lord, we both told Jenn we loved her and were proud of her—and heard in return her sincere, now indelibly engraved, "I love you." To our blessing, these were the last words we ever heard our daughter speak in life. They are not, thank God, the last communication we will ever have with her.

We depend on Tom for the rest of the drama. He recalls that Jenn talked on the telephone for a very long time with a former missionary companion from the Manchester, New Hampshire Mission. Consequently she was very tired the next morning when she went to work at 8:00 as a dental assistant in nearby Farmington. As the morning wore on, feeling increasingly ill, and more than weary, she telephoned Tom from work and asked him to bring to the dentist's office a longstanding medication which she had neglected to take. When he took by her medication on his way to class at Weber State, she said she felt "funny," and complained of flu-like symptoms, headache and general malaise. He advised her to go home if the illness continued, but she reminded him that she had scheduled an interview with an attorney as part of some research she was conducting for a term paper at the university. That was the last time Tom ever saw his wife alive.

Just before noon, Jenn told the doctor she would have to go home, and she left the office, apparently still hoping to be able to recover enough to conduct the interview later that day. At 12:35 Jennifer telephoned the veterinary office in Layton where Tom worked. The receptionist remembers that Jenn, crying and frantic, asked to speak to Tom, who was still en route from school. Jenn asked her to have Tom call immediately, and hung up.

On arriving at work in Layton at 1:15, Tom immediately telephoned home, but received no response. On hearing of her frantic state, a condition totally foreign to Jennifer, he was overcome by a sense of dread. He telephoned the dentist's office and learned that Jenn had left work about noon. Hoping that she had felt better and gone to her interview, he kept trying to telephone her, without success. The dread continued. At 2:15 he telephoned their neighbor in Bountiful and asked if their car was in the driveway. "It is," she reported; whereupon Tom told her of his concerns and asked her to go next door and check on Jennifer. The neighbor entered the apartment, found Jennifer dead, and called the paramedics, who worked with her to no avail, and pronounced her dead. The coroner later fixed the time of death at about 12:40, within moments of her call to Tom. The state examiner opined that severe retching and vomiting had induced a seizure and triggered the brain aneurism which killed her.

We are haunted yet by this thought: Jennifer, knowing that a medication she had been taking for several years could not be taken when pregnant, may have stopped taking it to surprise Tom and us with an announcement of pregnancy. Another image lingers in my memory of grief: Jennifer's bishop came through the viewing line and expressed his shock at her passing, which occurred the day before he was to call her to be the president of the young women in his ward. Thinking of what this would have meant to her and what it symbolized in her life, I choke up still, and think I always shall.

What We Learned from Our Daughter's Death

We live in the midst of death, the only species who understand that we will die. All religions undertake to explain the reasons for our lives and our deaths; and our cultures erect diverting facades and concoct pleasant fictions to shore us up against the impermanence, mutability, and dissolution of everything earthly. All of these placebos steel us against the fact that, as William Cullen Bryant wrote in "Thanatopsis":

> Yet a few days, and thee
> The all-beholding the sun shall see no more
> In all his course.[1]

Janice and I, like most mature human beings, were well-acquainted with the facts of life and death. We also had abiding faith in the eternal realities as taught and exemplified by Jesus Christ, Himself risen from the dead. In addition, we also benefitted from human medical knowledge, experience, and the law of averages—all of which enabled a modicum of expectation about how long we and ours could expect to live healthy and active lives. For us death was real, but it happened only to parents and relatives who had reached the harvest years. Death remained a distant and momentarily non-threatening abstraction.

Lulled by the cycles of nature and the routine of our days, we were not prepared to see our vital and vibrant young daughter lying before us in a coffin: stiff, cold and lifeless, and clad, ironically but suitably, in her wedding dress. We were not prepared to perform the rituals which we had expected she would one day perform in our behalf. We were not prepared for the way in which her death laid bare the falsehood that we who had generally been able to achieve what we went after were, after all, subject to uncontrollable and unseen powers, to fate, to what the ancients called *doom*.

In responding to Jennifer's sudden death, we are probably not very different from other believers who grieve. But telling how it was for us—groping for some degree of serenity and certitude, however fluctuating, amidst a willy-nilly and irrational life—may give readers support in their journeys through mortal mists. We want to share what we would have given anything to have gained otherwise than by the death of the apple of our eye and, with our two fine sons, more than a third of the joy and hope and promise of our lives. As fellow mourners in the household of the Saints, we would like to share some personal observations, insights, even inspiration which we have stored up in our souls during the most painful of mortal vicissitudes.

The Bell Tolls for Us

Through it all we never had the slightest worry about Jennifer's well-being. She, unlike us, was fine. At the moment of her death, the real Jennifer began a blessed continuation of life in another dimension and sphere, which despite some occasional hints remains essentially incomprehensible to us earthlings who momentarily remain ensconced in this earth/time warp and walk in faith the trembling plank of mortality. The assurance of eternal life—hers, ours, anyone's—never failed us throughout the experiences surrounding her death. This assurance came at once to us as a certitude, a conviction, and a higher reality, and it has so hovered in our souls ever since. That is the first given we learned. We have no doubts about Jennifer's state. We trust the Lord. Knowing she had made angelic mortal beginnings, been an obedient child and faithful woman, friend, missionary (official and unofficial), and loving wife, we knew she would make a lovely angel in eternity. We questioned only the timing.

It is clear to us now that it was not the eternalized Jennifer for whom we mourned and yet mourn. It was, instead, we whom we mourned. We mourned for the wrenching, abrupt, irrevocable end of our parental hopes and dreams, plans and expectations, for the end of things which now would never be. On that fatal day Jennifer returned, as Elder Neal A. Maxwell describes it, "to a home where the past, the present, and the future form an everlasting and eternal now!"[2] We, however, are temporarily confined to our shrunken and boundaried "mortal now" and the conditions of our second estate. Shortsighted as we are, we are permitted to grieve for our loss, our deprivation, our heartbreak. And we do. The effects linger for all time.

But working through our apprenticeship to the eternal perspective and learning to place in the perspective of eternity our mortal gains and losses clarifies our vision, fosters hope, increases faith in our God and the plan of salvation, and firms our commitment to an eternity in which we now have a very large stake in the presence there of our daughter, our dearest hostage to destiny. Until the great reunion, we still miss her, every day, every night. Thoughts and memories of her crowd our days, echo through our memories like a sigh, and are central to our hopes for the future, where she will remain an indelible part of us, in and out of time.

The Answer to the Question, "Why Me?"

As Janice and I tearfully embraced, just moments after the plank broke which was propping up our world, I started to whisper in her ear the cliché, "Why us?" In an instant I was flooded with the understanding that I knew why; I realized the wrongness of the cliché. Implicit in that "why me?" rhetorical question is not only foolish egotism, pride, and faithless misunderstanding of the plan of God, but the wrongheadedness of a debit-credit eternal accountancy which implies that we had somehow merited, through whatever imagined deeds, a waiver of the very tests and trials for which we agreed to come to Earth. The question also implies not only that we deserve the most felicitous of human destinies, but that we know, better than God, exactly what is best for us.

The Spirit chided me betimes, and I heard myself repeating to Janice the words which flashed into my mind: "Why not us? It's God's will; it's what we're here for." I explained my feelings and Janice, spiritual woman that she is, concurred at once. That insight, settling amidst our grief, has made all the difference. Throughout the whole ordeal of Jennifer's death, we have been buoyed up in the rough current of mortality by the sense of the Holy Spirit's sustaining presence, by the words of the Lord to the Prophet Joseph Smith, struggling with despair in Liberty Jail, that "all these things shall give thee experience, and shall be for thy good," and by the Lord's answer to Joseph's pained outcry (and to my unuttered question), "The Son of Man hath descended below them all. Art thou greater than he?"(D&C 122:7–8).

"Thy Will Be Done in Earth, As It Is in Heaven" (Matthew 6:10)

To a missionary in Switzerland frustrated by the perceived failure of the Lord to give him baptisms when he had dotted every moral and spiritual *i* and crossed every *t* of obedience and effort, I said:

> Learn to mean what you say when you pray, "Thy will be done." Learn to put yourself in the hands of the Lord; be His tool; allow him to do with you as He desires. Don't counsel Him on what He wishes. Be at the ready for His use. Then you'll truly be God's man in Zürich, living at His beck and call, ready, when He asks you, to jump, and, jumping, asking Him, "how high?" on the way up.

This inspired counsel helped me as much as that young man. However large my shortfall and however age has crimped my high jump, the will to do His will is there. That will is key to healing the disconsolate soul.

Torn as we are in mortality between the demands of the weak flesh and the compulsions of an independent spirit, it is not easy to surrender our wills, in faith, to the will of God. Death is a schoolmaster which humbles and purifies and prepares us for submission to our God as nothing else can. Out of death-induced humility arises dependence upon our Father and freedom from reliance upon the arm of flesh. Jesus, again the model of humble submission, told His disciples near the pool of Bethesda, "I can of mine own self do nothing,"—"I seek," He revealed, "not mine own will, but the will of the Father which hath sent me"(John 5:30).

Overriding our own mortal wills and desires, our Father chose to fold Jennifer into eternity, according to His timetable and not ours. It is for us to bow our souls before the chastening rod, to cry with Jesus in Gethsemane, "O my Father, if this cup may not pass away from me, except I drink it, *thy will be done*"(Matthew 26:42; emphasis added). Such submission to the Father's will, in faith that, as Lehi proclaimed, "all things have been done in the wisdom of him who knoweth all things"(2 Nephi 2:24), is a major step in fulfilling our mortal apprenticeships and mourning our dead in a manner which reflects our faith. It is learning to say, with Jesus, "into thy hands I commend my spirit"(Luke 23:46). The trick, of course, is leaving it there.

The Difference Between Being a Victim and Being a Submissive Servant

During those first dark days of distress after our daughter's passing, we felt, for the first time in our lives, like victims. We did not enjoy the feeling of being at the mercy of an apparently feckless and irrational fate or power which, hitherto benign, suddenly seemed, if not malignant, certainly unfeeling. Occasionally we felt like puppets controlled from the wings. Nor did we, proud souls, like being pitied by others. As time passed, this sense of victimhood mocked our attempts to ignore our impotence and vulnerability before an unseen, irrational fate.

Battered, we stood naked before our God and the realities of our fallen mortal condition. Pondering our place in His plan, we realized that men and women could live like victims, enjoying others' momentary pity and fearing the next willy-nilly blows of fate, or they could live as Promethean heroes, accepting, engaging, and battling the vultures of life. The Lord's way became clear to us: faithfully submit, watch, pray, and be "anxiously engaged" in exercising our agency so long as we have life. "For the power," we read, is inherent in us; "wherein [we] are agents unto [ourselves]"(D&C 58:28). This doctrine tastes good; and we had always so believed.

We also realized that the chastening of the Lord is tangible evidence of His hand in refining our souls and fitting us out for the kingdom. As young missionaries in Switzerland, my companion and I were attacked by a bear of a man who had been commanded by the Virgin Mary, he said, to kill us. He tried and we fled, the assailant running after us with pruning shears. We ran to a cruelly unsympathetic traffic cop who waved off our complaint with the admonition to "go home, where you belong, and leave the Swiss people alone." Feeling victimized and persecuted, we rode home, where I telephoned President Jesse R. Curtis and indignantly explained what had occurred. I waited breathlessly, envisioning his raising his arm to the square and calling down thunder and lightning upon the Swiss nation, and, in particular, the canton of Argan and the township of Umiken.

Instead the president chuckled and said words that occurred to me in our mourning: "Elder Cracroft, how the Lord must love you!" To my "huh?" he quoted Revelations 3:19, "As many as I love, I rebuke and chasten." In our struggle to regain our accustomed spiritual/mortal equilibrium, Janice and I came to consider ourselves recipients of our Father's rebuking and chastening "tough love," which occasioned much-needed refinement, unfortunately a job not yet half done.

Throughout our ordeal the words of the psalmist have reverberated through our souls: "The Lord is my shepherd, I shall not want. . . . Yea, though I walk through the valley of the shadow of death, I will fear no evil: for thou art with me; *thy rod and thy staff they comfort me*" (Psalm 23:1,4; emphasis added). We have learned, in our small and faltering way, to see the grace and mercy in, and cherish the comfort of the rod and staff of the Good Shepherd, and increasingly we have gained confidence in the promise of the psalm's closing line: "Surely goodness and mercy shall follow me all the days of my life: and I will dwell in the house of the Lord for ever"(6).

Expressions of Sympathy and Acts of Kindness Are Welcome and Essential to Our Spiritual and Emotional Recovery

Neither of us had understood, before receiving hundreds of family members, friends, and associates at the mortuary and in the Provo Bonneville First Ward Relief Society room, how important to us would be this gathering of friends, how crucial would be our hearing their outpourings of sympathy. We have always tried to attend to the passing of relatives, dear friends, and colleagues, but now we know how important others' expressions are to the spiritual and emotional well-being of the grieving family. We know that those who come leave the viewing basically unaffected by our grief and return to life as usual. Life goes on. But how much we appreciated their taking time, as Alma admonished the newly baptized saints at the Waters of Mormon, "to mourn with those that mourn; yea, and comfort those that stand in need of comfort"(Mosiah 18:9). Janice and I, Tom, our sons Richard and Jeffrey and their wives, were remarkably uplifted by the host of willing Saints—and not a few ain'ts—who rallied to our sides.

We were blessed by all who asked "is there anything we can do for you?" but even more blessed by those who did what they could do, unbidden—arranging flowers, bringing in meals, preparing and serving the luncheon for a large number of guests, and, in the case of Elma Mack our neighbor, that enduring act of transcribing on diskette the entire funeral service. So many blessed our lives by their awareness of the mighty change that had occurred in the Cracrofts' lives. And we were profoundly encouraged by those whose services continued even after the conclusion of public mourning. We appreciated the ongoing inquiries by solicitous friends, neighbors, and ward members. My sister Helen led the list. She not only spoke at the funeral, but she talked with Janice by telephone from Bountiful, Texas, or wherever she was, virtually every single day for the next six months. She strengthened Janice and me as no one else could have done. Through all of this outpouring, we got a glimpse of what it means to be charitable.

Conversely—and Janice asks that I make this point—people need to understand that to avoid any reference to the passing of a loved one is, to the grieving individuals, hurtful and puzzling. It hurts to have a friend who has failed, for whatever well-meaning reason, to acknowledge that a portion of our souls has suddenly been eclipsed. All that is necessary is a handshake and a heartfelt "I'm sorry." It is petty, I know, but amidst all of the outpouring of kindness at the passing of our daughter, the few who have never acknowledged our loss seem to linger in our memories. Remember: talking to bereaved parents about their loss is a welcome sign that others feel and understand and sympathize.

This is a universal fact. Not long ago, while my wife and I were attending a scholarly gathering at another school, we saw a long-time professional acquaintance and his wife. Aware that this couple had lost their son three months earlier in an avalanche, and noting that they seemed distant and distracted, I expressed our sorrow and sympathy on their son's passing. Instantly they became animated, and Janice shared with them our own forever recent loss. Oh, how they wanted to talk about their loss. Oh, how they wanted the world to recognize that they had been shorn of a vital part of their lives. They poured out their grief, taking comfort in speaking with others who seemed to understand. However well-meant your avoidance of a painful subject, remember that to avoid acknowledging another's pain may well be seen as ignoring and somehow discounting that pain. Say something; don't worry about awkwardness or intrusion.

And some converse counsel to mourners: part of your apprenticeship is learning not to magnify perceived slights, which generally occur out of timidity, fear, or the desire to help you preserve your privacy.

Our God Whispers Comfort and Assurance to Our Souls. We Are Not Left Alone.

The reality of our Father's outreach and embrace is seldom more meaningful than in a time of loss. Throughout the dark night and into the gradual dawning of a brighter day, the words of the holy scriptures came unbidden to comfort us. The hymns of Zion took on new significance, admonishing us that "Though deepening trials throng your way, Press on, press on, ye Saints of God!"[3] and calling:

> Come, ye disconsolate, where'er ye languish;
> Come to the mercy seat, fervently kneel.
> Here bring your wounded hearts; here tell your anguish.
> Earth has no sorrow that heav'n cannot heal.[4]

and answering the question, in the words of our friend, Emma Lou Thayne, who knows a thing or two about grief, "Where can I turn for peace? Where is my solace," with:

> He answers privately, Reaches my reaching
> In my Gethsemane, Savior and Friend.
> Gentle the peace he finds for my beseeching.
> Constant he is and kind, Love without end.[5]

From the pulpit we heard the plan of God preached by the Saints, as if for the first time. The talks at Jennifer's funeral service were enormously comforting. It was at that service that Elder Neal A. Maxwell reminded us, in his felicitous combination of spirit and words, of things we needed to hear—and which continue to refresh us years afterward. He said:

> When we have pain in the present, which is certainly understandable today, it brings one in memory of the Prophet Joseph Smith's interesting and profound statement about how in the presence of God all things past, present, and future are combined into an Eternal Now. As I think about Heavenly Father's Eternal Now, it is very different from our Now. In our Now we have a kind of glimpse of things in which there is an optical outcome in which we see the things of the moment magnified, and the things of eternity are blurred and diminished, unless we have faith, which obviously the people of this congregation have.
>
> Heavenly Father asks us to trust, as we can see Tom doing, in Heavenly Father's Eternal Now, because He sees things we do not see. That is what he means when we are asked to look at things with the eyes of faith, and then we see things as they really are. . . . [Remember], it is Heavenly Father's timetable, not ours. [6]

As is sometimes the case, our Heavenly Father reassured Tom of Jennifer's blessed state through granting him a night-long conversation with his late wife. Our Father has reassured my grieving Janice in several dreams and visions regarding Jenn's activity in the Spirit World, and He has, through the intercession of a former missionary associate in Zürich, vividly refocused my own vision. It happened like this:

In January 1994, on the day after our daughter's death, I received a letter from a former Swiss-Austrian missionary living in Salt Lake City. Unaware of our sorrow he wrote that he had recently seen my name on an article and was writing to inquire if I were the same Elder Cracroft he had known in Zürich in 1958, at the beginning of his mission and near the end of mine. He said he had been deeply impressed by a story I had recounted at a missionary conference about losing and recovering a contact lens. He had, he wrote, related the incident often over the years and hoped he had told the story accurately. He then repeated the story as he recalled it. Although I had not told the story in some years, I was amazed that he had captured it exactly as I recollected it.

Briefly, I had told how my very serious visual problems had been instantly corrected by the purchase in Zürich of corneal contact lenses. Because I was so thrilled with my newfound vision, I was greatly stunned when, the following week, while tracting on a hillside on a rainy afternoon, I had been forced by a bit of dust to take out my right contact lens. As I was re-inserting the lens, a sudden gust of wind blew the lens from my finger. After futilely searching for twenty minutes on hands and knees on the wet gravel road, I asked my companion, Elder Reading, to join me in prayer. I pled with the Lord; I reasoned with Him; I pointed out that we had several important discussions scheduled for that evening; I noted that I could see nothing to be gained by withholding the whereabouts of the lens and everything to be gained by our finding it. After all, the work of the ministry was at stake.

As I said "Amen," and arose to my feet, I knew through what Joseph Smith called "flashes of intelligence" just what I must do. I explained to my companion, who stayed on his knees, shaking his head at my plan. I took out the left lens, thereby plunging myself into virtual blindness. I wet the lens, held it on my fingertip, and waited. In a moment another gust of wind swept the left lens from my finger, and I stood there, seeing only a blur, my heart in my throat, and pled with my companion not to lose sight of the left lens floating on the breeze. On his knees, he followed the airborne lens for some twelve feet and, it seemed, twenty minutes, then exclaimed, "It's falling," as it began to sink to the ground.

"Do you still see it?" I implored.

"I see it," he said. Then silence. Fear. Unbearable tension. Then: "Oh my gosh. . . . It's landed almost right on top of the other lens."

Still virtually blind, I gingerly crawled over to my companion, who cautiously restored both of my lenses, my seer stones, my Urim and Thummim, which I inserted: "And there was light!" We knelt again, and, full of gratitude, I thanked our God for tender mercies; and, rising, we pressed on to the next house, filled with wonder at a God who knows each sparrow's fall *and* the exact whereabouts in Switzerland of Elder Cracroft's right—and left—contact lenses.[7]

There it was, my contact lens story, untold in many years, suddenly resounding in my soul, thirty-six years later, arriving via U.S. mail at the darkest moment of our lives. Janice and I knew we had received a message from the Lord. He had reminded us in no uncertain terms that He was there with us at the fall of our dear sparrow, just as He had been there with me on that long-ago hillside. The Lord, who knows Alpha from Omega, beginnings and endings, was deftly pointing out that our Jennifer's death was merely another event in our salvation journey; and that all things, including Jennifer and Tom and Janice and me, were in His hands.

We have learned that our Father will use every means to encourage us; we need only request, expect, listen, and discern. And the revelation will come, often through others, and often in unexpected ways. And we have also learned, mortal as we are, that we always hope for just a bit more.

The Saving Vision of the Eternal Perspective

I close with another death. My father, Ralph Cracroft, nearly sixty-three years old and blind for the previous twelve years, died of cancer on March 26, 1960. Janice and I, with my mother, Grace, and my dear Aunt Florence, stood by his bedside and watched his life ebb away. At the moment of his passing, I put my arms around my mother and prepared for the plunge into the abyss. But the abyss did not gape. As we embraced I suddenly had one of those "flashes of intelligence" and saw my father, alive and seeing and happy, in another place. The vision was fleeting, but it was so true that I burst into spontaneous testimony to Mom, Florie, Janice, and the Holy Spirit, who was there: "Dad is alive; he's still living!" I had been flooded with the eternal perspective; I knew Dad had joyfully entered the

Eternal Room, and I knew that all was well with him—and, it must follow, with us. I learned in a flash that the belly of the whale is a temporary mortal phase and not a lasting condition, for Heavenly Father had just shown me the way out. I knew it was so.

When Jonah found himself micro-managed by the Lord into the dark "belly of hell" of the big fish, where "the waters compassed me about, even to the soul: the depth closed me round about," he came to the same conclusion as would Alma, and as did we, and cried, "I will look again toward thy holy temple. . . . When my soul fainted within me I remembered the Lord: and my prayer came in unto thee, into thine holy temple" (Jonah 2:5–7). The Lord sent salvation and plucked His reluctant servant from the belly of the whale: "And the Lord spake unto the fish, and it vomited out Jonah upon the dry land" (Jonah 2:1–10).

Here is the truth about whale bellies: after few or many days, the Lord, having tried us in the very depths of adversity, will deliver us out of darkness into light. All who have lost loved ones (and who has not?) will come to know, even amidst the ordeal, that "the light shineth in darkness; and the darkness comprehended it not" (John 1:5). This light is from God, and "that which is of God is light; and he that receiveth light, and continueth in God, receiveth more light; and that light groweth brighter and brighter until the perfect day"(D&C 50:24). We are full of gratitude for Him who lights our way out of mortal whale bellies and restores our eternal perspective.

Life Goes On

Through this mortal ordeal and struggle toward the light, Janice and I have felt, still feel, and will doubtless always feel the mortal ache that accompanies loss. We feel keenly the shrinking of our world, being deprived of our daughter's presence, the absence of her faithful, enthusiastic, cheerful, happy, witty, exciting, and unique self. We feel, always, the absence of what might have been and the longing for what will never be—at least in life as we now know it. In every prayer we still pray for her, bless her in her present state, thank our God for her life.

Our apprenticeship in the eternal perspective is not over. Our

Heavenly Father continues to school Janice and me, as He does all, in every age, in every condition, who seek the Lord. I, of course, am just about perfect (though some question my humility); Janice, of course, has a ways to go. Our Father gives, in so many ways, His ringing affirmative answer to Job's question, "If a man die, shall he live again?" (Job 14:14). His resounding "Yes" to that question has become so central to our world view that we are often impatient with mortality and long for the perfect and immortal day.

Meanwhile, life goes on. We no longer expect cannon salutes or international tributes in recognition of our daughter's passing. Outwardly, at least, little has changed. We have learned that routines and dailinesses restore, that work engages and engrosses, that the best defense against mortal mutability is to be "anxiously engaged" in establishing Zion, that we are at our best when we remove our fingers from our own pulses, when we lose ourselves in larger-than-I ventures and when we finally stop singing the popular Italian aria, "Me, Me, Me, Me, Me!"

As we engage, life becomes endurable; thoughts about the departed come only several times a day instead of every minute. All about us children and grandchildren are born, grow into adults, marry, beget children, grow old, and die in the Lord. Every one of them undergoes what we have experienced and, if believing, learns what we have learned. We understand, at last, that through all of the seasons of mortality we have been steadily and unfailingly enriched by our loss and by our apprenticeship to immortality. Meanwhile, the ache continues. Oh, how we miss our baby girl.

NOTES

1. William Cullen Bryant, "Thanatopsis," *The Norton Anthology of American Literature*, Fourth Edition Shorter (New York: W. W. Norton & Company, 1995), pp. 423–24.

2. Neal A. Maxwell, *Men and Women of Christ* (Salt Lake City: Bookcraft, 1991), p. 51.

3. Eliza R. Snow, "Though Deepening Trials," *Hymns*, no. 122.

4. Thomas Moore, "Come, Ye Disconsolate," *Hymns*, no. 115.

5. Emma Lou Thayne, "Where Can I Turn for Peace?" *Hymns*, no. 129.

6. Neal A. Maxwell, from the funeral services for Jennifer Cracroft Lewis, January 29, 1994.

7. See Richard H. Cracroft, "Divine Designs: Tracing the Lord's 'Pattern in All Things'," *BYU Speeches, 1996–97* (Provo: Brigham Young University, 1997), pp. 124–25.

Chapter Four

WAITING FOR LIFE
by Ardith Walker

Life was perfect. Things were going just as Steve and I had planned way back in 1959 when we were seniors in high school, first falling in love. We would sit in the old green rockers on my back porch and talk about the future and all that it held for us. Just as we planned on those moonlit nights, I had waited for Steve while he was on his mission. I considered it my mission too. We had certain days each month we would fast together, and I faithfully read my scriptures. To keep my spirits high I got two little jars which I used to count down the days Steve was gone. In one jar I put a dime each morning and watched it get fuller and fuller. In the other jar I had 731 red hots, and each evening I would eat one. As the dimes grew and the red hots disappeared I could see the realities of our dreams coming closer. Finally those red hots were gone, and I went with Steve's family to pick him up from his mission.

A few months later we had a fairy tale wedding in Steve's backyard with yellow roses to match the bright yellow dresses of my seven bridesmaids. Our wedding cake was a replica of the Salt Lake Temple. We had friends sing our favorite love songs throughout the evening, and we were so happy I didn't even notice that it rained for several minutes right in the middle of the reception.

Now I was teaching school as we dreamed I would be, while Steve was a year ahead of schedule getting his degree at BYU. When

---

Ardith Walker *and her husband, Steve, finally had three children, just five short of their goal. Ardith enjoys teaching first grade, loves playing with her four beautiful granddaughters, and marvels more and more at the advent of life.*

we were dating we had talked about how many children we would like and had agreed that eight would be perfect—four girls and four boys. We had been married a little over a year when, continuing right along the idyllic path of our life together, we found out the glorious news: I was pregnant.

This would be no ordinary baby. This would be ours. Our child would never spit up and rarely cry. Our baby would be born with a full head of hair, reciting the ABC's at six months. On the way home from the doctor's office we stopped at Christensen's Department Store and bought a package of tiny white undershirts. I opened them up in the car and imagined how it was going to feel coming home from the hospital with a beautiful bright-eyed little baby wearing one of those cute little shirts.

We wanted to announce our exciting news with a flair so that everyone could feel our joy. With December just around the corner, we parodied "Christmas is coming and the goose is getting fat."

> Christmas is coming
> and Ardith's getting fat.
> Oh, my goodness gracious
> What do you think of that!

We planned to sing to my family first, then Steve's. We even practiced with the guitar, a guitar I had bought for Steve with the dimes I saved during his mission. But the bleeding started before we got to sing.

The announcement of our pregnancy abruptly changed from singing to frantically asking my mom if we could borrow the bedpan. It seemed impossible for anything to be marring our long-awaited dream; I was sure we could fix it. When Dr. Thomson told me to stay down I obeyed: I didn't even get up to use the bathroom. I not only stayed down, I stayed flat.

But it wasn't flat enough. The following night the cramping turned into contractions, the bleeding became severe, and Steve, acting as doctor, nurse, comforter, and caretaker, helped me through the agonizing ordeal of miscarrying our hope of a new life, our song in the making. This was not the way it was supposed to happen.

At first I was relieved to go to the hospital where I would be in professional hands. Steve looked even more relieved. He took the contents of the night before and my possibilities of motherhood in a bag as we'd been instructed. The best bag we could find was a plastic produce bag from Reams. An intern on call took it and left the room. When he returned he said, "Next time you won't need to bring in all the tissue—just the fetus. Put everything on the counter and if a fork slices through it discard that part."

I was admitted to the maternity ward. Although they were careful to put me in a private room, the reality of our loss was magnified when I saw my friend Anne being wheeled down the hall on her way to deliver a hefty, healthy son. Later that day when I ventured out of my room a well-meaning visitor asked me which baby was mine.

Even things that normally would have made us laugh didn't. When Steve called Dr. Thomson's office at 11:00 the night before to tell them I was miscarrying, he accidently dialed the wrong number and got our neighbor Ruth Shoell. Thinking he was talking to a nurse he carefully explained the miscarriage in explicit detail. Sister Shoell listened patiently, then expressed her concern. When Steve realized he wasn't talking to a nurse but to a ward member he was too embarrassed to explain his mistake, thanked her for her time, hung up and put his head in his hands. She must have thought Steve was calling everyone in the ward just to let them know. He might as well have. Losing the baby felt that cosmic.

As soon as we got home from the hospital I took the little undershirts we had draped over our dresser mirror, carefully folded them, and put them in the bottom drawer. I lay down on my bed and sobbed myself to sleep. The hard part was waking up to the reality of nothingness, the emptiness, the loneliness, the awfulness. I wanted to sleep and sleep and sleep.

The family, the ward, my schoolteaching friends were all loving and supportive. I appreciated that they asked how I was doing. I appreciated more that they listened. It was helpful to hear about others' miscarriages because I realized that I wasn't alone. But even the help could hurt. A few made unintentionally hurtful comments about miscarriage being no big deal. One referred to it as a "little mishap." A member of the bishopric wondered how I was doing after the "incident."

Sister Hardman, an elderly neighbor who had been a birthing nurse years earlier, advised me to take it easy so I could get pregnant again quickly. And that's what I wanted. It wasn't long until I could feel others were as anxious for us to get pregnant again as we were. I was sure that our plans had merely been interrupted and that in no time we would be right back on track. I thought, we may have to change the timing of our song to an Easter song, but we will soon be singing nonetheless.

But spring came and went. A second pregnancy wasn't turning out to be quite as simple as we had planned. I found myself watching my friend Anne's baby out of the corner of my eye every Sunday at church—noticing how pudgy and cute and alive he was. They sat just a few rows in front of us on Mother's Day. My heart ached for our little miscarried child. I wondered where he was, if he'd grown, what he was doing, who was holding him. The Sunday School begonia plant did not make up for the loss.

At the end of that school year I quit teaching so I could settle down, concentrate, and put all my energies into getting pregnant again. In retrospect, I should have kept working. I had way too much time to think. Getting pregnant became the most important thing in my world.

After a year of trying and crying I started going to a fertility specialist. We tried many treatments, from taking my temperature each morning before I got out of bed—even buying a new thermometer because I was sure the first one wasn't working—to lying in a cold room on a cold table enduring a cold scope during a colposcopic exam, to testing to see if the sperm were alive and well, to having extensive four-hour surgery for endometriosis. With each new treatment my hopes would soar, only to be dashed a few weeks later.

Infertility doesn't seem like much of a problem until you experience it. I could never understand why those Old Testament women in Genesis and Judges got so upset about being barren. "Give me children or I die" seemed melodramatic. But not having life in the first place can be like losing life. Experiencing infertility has too much in common with having a miscarriage. In some ways it may be harder. The sense of loss each month, the hope dissolved again, the empty arms, were all stark reminders that we were still not parents, our song unsung.

During the second year of infertility I became desperate. I was obsessed with having a baby. My self-worth became dependent on being able to conceive and bear a child. I was constantly reading articles and books about the signs of pregnancy. I spent hours looking in the mirror to see if the whites of my eyes were somewhat gray or if the freckles over my nose might be the mask of pregnancy. I would check my chest to see if it was tender yet, and concentrated hard to see if maybe I really could be a little nauseated.

Sometimes people who didn't know our situation would ask why we were waiting so long to have children. One fertile relative jokingly asked if we knew "how to do it." I noticed ward members and friends glance at my stomach to see how things were coming. Every time I bought a new dress I had to make sure it fit snugly so no one would mistake it for a maternity smock.

My entire world focused on pregnancy. Everyone was pregnant: fat people, skinny people, ugly people, people with acne, people who smoked, people who didn't deserve to have kids, people too young, people too old, people who already had way too many kids, people who didn't even want a baby. I think for a while just about everyone I saw was either pregnant, had just had a baby, or was going to be pregnant the next day. Everyone but me.

Steve was elder's quorum president in a ward made up mostly of young married couples. I was often called on to take dinner to new parents or to do their laundry or ironing. Once when I asked if there was anything else I could do I ended up defrosting a freezer. But vacuuming other women's floors so they could hold their babies got me absolutely zero blessings in heaven. Most often I performed those compassionate services out of pure duty, duty filled with more self-pity and hurt than love. The part I hated most was when the new parents would proudly show me their baby. I would smile and ooh and aah on the outside, while on the inside all I felt was pain. They seemed to expect me to be excited to hold their baby. I didn't want to hold their baby. I wanted to hold my baby.

I felt resentful when these new parents would bear their testimonies, saying how thankful they were that God had loved and trusted them enough to give them this child. I started feeling as if God must give babies as a reward for righteousness. What were we doing wrong? Why wasn't God rewarding us? Didn't He trust us with a baby?

I would often be jarred awake in the dark hours of the morning by the stark realization that I still hadn't had a baby. I would lay there in the blackness overwhelmed by the sickening thought of how old I was getting. First it was twenty-five. Then twenty-six. Then twenty-seven. I was aging steadily, and still no baby.

While not working I had plenty of time to read the big Walker family history book which included nearly everyone in Pleasant Grove. I studied the genealogy sheets in the book to see how many months after marriage first babies were born. Either Pleasant Grove environment shortens the length of gestation or there was a surprisingly high number of shotgun weddings. It made me mad that Steve and I had been so "righteous." I wished we had had to get married.

One night as Steve said our prayer he told God, as usual, that we would like to have a baby "if it be Thy will." When he finished praying I angrily told him not to say "if it be Thy will" anymore as it just undid all the good of my prayers. I wanted to have a baby now. I could no longer wait for God's will.

I can't remember having time to read the scriptures—I was too busy researching the Walker family history book. But a few days after my outburst during family prayer I came upon the scripture in Proverbs 3:5: "Trust in the Lord with all thine heart; and lean not unto thine own understanding." I'm sure I had read that verse before, but this time it seemed to stand out. This time the words seared me.

I printed that scripture on an index card and stuck it on our dresser mirror. Peace seeped into me—not dramatically, but little by little. Slowly the worthless and panicky feeling of desperation to have a baby left. It felt so good to have that feeling leave. Sometimes the peace was fleeting, and when life would start to feel heavy again I would go into our bedroom and read and reread that index card so I could once again tune into the peace I had felt.

I put the Walker family history book away, signed up for some classes at BYU, and started substitute teaching. But the best thing we did to secure the peaceful feeling was to apply to become adoptive parents. It was an interesting process. Previously, whenever I thought of adopting I felt that we would be giving up. But after the peaceful feeling came it felt more like, "We're not giving up. We're just going about it in a different way."

Once our adoption papers were processed I felt a new zest for living. For the first time in a long while I actually felt joy. I made baby clothes and decorated the baby's room. I put those little undershirts in the top drawer. Instead of reading *Signs of Pregnancy* I read *How to Raise a Brighter Child.*

Our adoption papers had been in almost a year and were due to be processed any day when I realized I was two weeks late. This had happened several times before, so when we went into Salt Lake City for our adoption appointment I stopped in at Dr. Hall's for a progesterone shot to get me regulated. He checked me first. Lo and behold he told us I was really, truly, actually pregnant.

We were so overwhelmed and so overjoyed and so befuddled that when we went back to the adoption agency to tell them the news, Steve stammered to the receptionist, "We would like to talk to somebody about something." The adoption agency assured us we would be on the top of the list if anything were to go wrong. On the way home from Salt Lake City I bawled because I had been planning on bringing our adopted baby home any day and now we would have to wait again. But by the time we got home the thrill of being pregnant filled me with such joy I could scarcely contain myself. I draped the little undershirts back over our dresser mirror.

Those years when I finally put my trust in the Lord were some of the best years of my life. It was during this time that Steve and I became especially good friends. In retrospect I can see that if things hadn't turned out as they did we probably never would have thought of going to Harvard, which in turn allowed us to live a year in England on a study abroad program.

Sometimes we are so close to situations that we are blinded by our own shortsightedness. Anxious as I was for a baby, I realize now that it may have been better to wait. Death is not a good thing. Infertility is not a good thing. But God can use both to help us achieve good things.

I know that if we had never had any children my life could have been rich had I kept that trust in the Lord. That little index card with the scripture printed on it stayed on our dresser mirror for years. I still have it. The ink has faded, the card has yellowed, but the peace from those words deepens.

With or without miscarriage, with or without babies, life's a lot better for me when I trust in the Lord with all my heart and lean not unto my own understanding. In the middle of May, six years after we were married, I finally held our first child in my arms. The only song I could think of to sing as a lullaby was "Christmas is coming and I am getting fat. Oh my goodness gracious, what do you think of that!" Our baby wore those cute little undershirts all summer, even when it was way too hot.

CLARA MARIE
by Candace Kennard

It seems the day it happened was a warm, beautiful, spring afternoon. But I realize as I read my journal again that it was the end of January, not warm at all.

January 22, 1984

Mom called today to tell me that Grammie Rene had died at 9:00 A.M. She died fairly quickly, without much pain. Mom said the funeral would be Tuesday the 24th. She and Dad said I shouldn't come because I'm so far along. But I missed Grandma Koster's funeral and I want to be with family.

January 24

After the funeral Mom and I were sitting at her kitchen table chatting when I felt the baby kick. It was so violent that it made me sit straight up in my chair.

January 26

We got home about 6:00 P.M. after a not-so-great trip home. Keith threw up all over the back seat. There was no rest stop for two hours so I awkwardly leaned over my seat to clean up as best I could. When I settled back into my seat I was surprised that the baby was so

---

Candace Kennard *married Kim Kennard in 1974. They and their eight children call American Fork home. At the time of these journal entries they made their home in Blanding, Utah. They have also lived in Tokyo and in Cardston, Raymond, and Arrowwood, Canada.*

still. With all of the jostling around, the baby must have been lulled to sleep inside me.

January 28

I got up bright and early and got the car ready to go to my sister's. Since it was an hour and a half to the doctor's office, we scheduled our prenatal appointments together so that we could watch each other's kids. Hers was a six-week check with her doctor, mine a thirty-eight-week check with my midwife.

Pat was her cheerful, happy self. She measured me and listened for the baby's heartbeat, listened and listened and couldn't hear anything, so I did some pelvic rocks and walked around. Then Pat tried to get a response by pushing against my belly back and forth. There was no reaction. There was no kicking back. Pat asked me when I last felt the baby move, and I remembered sitting at my mother's kitchen table. At that moment I knew for certain that the baby was not alive.

It was like having a terrible dream come true, one of those crazy dreams you have when you're pregnant. This pregnancy I had dreamed that Kim and I were in a swimming pool with a lot of his family. I asked where Keith was. Our eyes looked all around, then at the same time we both looked towards the deep end of the pool. Suddenly there was no water surrounding the drain—only Keith's naked little body, face down. Strangely we didn't run to resuscitate him, just knelt by him and prayed. I woke with a start. The dream stayed with me the entire day, I was so afraid something would happen to Keith. Could the dream have been about this baby?

When Pat could find no heart tones, we held each other and cried. I went into the other room and told JoRene. She said she thought everything would be all right. I believed her, even though I knew the baby was dead. She took the kids while I called Kim. He wasn't home. I left a message with his office that there was a problem with the baby and he needed to meet us at the hospital. Pat brought me to Dr. Cullum's. Pat talked with the nurses and the receptionist, paving the way for me so that I wouldn't have to deal with any of it. Dr. Cullum did an ultrasound and Pat explained to me what I was seeing. It looked like nothing to me. Dr. Cullum verified that there was no pulsing of the heart.

He told me I had three alternatives. I could go home and have Pat deliver the baby whenever I went into labor. I could try to spur on labor by intensive walking while staying near the hospital. Or they could give me a hormonal suppository to quicken the process. I didn't like any of the choices. I wanted to be put in the hospital, be completely knocked out, and have the baby taken out of me. Thankfully, Pat convinced me otherwise. Since I was already dilated to three centimeters she insisted that labor was imminent. With a brisk walk and some castor oil we could get things underway. In a trance, I submitted to her encouragement. As I got dressed, alone in the examining room, I felt unpregnant, very alone, and lonesome for Kim.

Pat explained some of the things I needed to think about, like the mortuary. Dr. Cullum called them. They said they would pick up the baby as soon as it had been delivered. When I came out, I was glad to see JoRene and the kids in the waiting room. I told her the baby was not alive and that I would probably deliver some time that night. We cried and hugged each other. When Kim walked in he held me, but didn't seem too upset. Could no one feel my pain?

At dinnertime Pat kept trying to talk me into Mexican food. She made me walk. She gave me the castor oil. I felt protected with Pat as my advocate. I couldn't take care of myself. I didn't know what to do. I was in a haze, with no direction. Pat was my guardian angel—guiding me, coaching me, leading me, encouraging me. I can't imagine having gone through this without Pat. She was with me every second. I knew this wasn't just a job to her; she cared, deeply and personally. Yet she was professional enough that she could be objective—she could make the decisions we weren't capable of making.

Our walk was brisk in the cold night air. We talked about everything and nothing, laughing one minute, crying the next. In this in-between waiting time, we walked, arm in arm, building up enough strength in my heart to be able to endure what was to come. By the time we got back to the hospital my water had broken. As I got out of my wet clothes and into a hospital gown I could feel my labor starting. When I got settled into bed, Kim and Harvey gave me a blessing, another nudge forward. But I was already exhausted, both physically and emotionally. I wanted to deal with labor and birth tomorrow. How would I find the strength to do this?

I did not want to deliver this baby. There would be no reward at the end of all that effort. Another mother in the next room to mine had just given birth, and I heard her baby cry. I felt an urge to see the child, not to hold it but to see what my baby could have looked like. Then the grief was too huge for me to face. Maybe it would just go away. I wanted to wake up and have it all over with.

Pat brought me lots of juice. She kept coaxing me to drink, telling me I could do it. She said we were almost there, I'd nearly made it through. I could give this last gift to my baby—I could deliver her body into this world. Before I knew it, Dr. Cullum was telling me to push. Somehow I knew I could do it. There was no turning back now. I pushed without much determination. I tried again, harder. I hadn't realized how much a baby helps in its own delivery. I had to do all of the work alone.

Finally I pushed with all the strength I could muster and out came her head. Soon her whole body was out, and they announced she was a beautiful baby girl. They wiped her off and cut the cord and laid her in a blanket by me. All the nurses who came in acted like everything was normal. Someone brought in a camera and took pictures of her. The thought of doing such a thing would never have occurred to me, but it felt right. The nurses would touch the baby and comment on how pretty she was—what an angel. Their unexpected actions were profoundly touching to me. How did they know to be so compassionate? Did they know how much easier their natural way made the experience for me?

They called the bishop. He came, even though it was nearly 2:00 A.M. He gave her a name and a blessing: Clara Marie. I didn't know if we'd be allowed to do that. I'm so glad we could—it made her seem more real, like she was an actual person.

After everyone left I held her in my arms and cried. I looked at every inch of her, unwrapping her blanket to see and to touch all of her. I stroked her tiny fingers and held her little foot in the palm of my hand. I rubbed her legs, caressed her arms. I remember touching her cheeks and noticing the dimple in her chin like all of my other babies. The softness of her skin melted into mine. This was my one chance to have my baby near, to know who she was, to experience her. Holding her perfect form I couldn't imagine what could have gone wrong with her. I talked to her, asked her why she couldn't stay. Was I not worthy?

I felt guilty for not being able to stay up for every minute of that one night. I finally had to lay her in the isolette so that I could sleep a couple of hours. When I woke it was early morning. I went over to her and held her, asking her again why she couldn't stay with me. I woke up Kim so that he could share this with us, be together in the peaceful morning hours. I'm so glad that no one came in, that they gave us time alone.

The time came that I feared most—the good-bye, allowing her to be taken for an autopsy and then to the mortuary. I hugged her and kissed her, then handed her to the nurse. Kim and I lay together and hugged each other until we heard from the pathologist with the autopsy results. They found no problems other than the umbilical cord having two vessels instead of three. Lots of babies are born with only two vessels and survive, so it must have been a cord accident. Somehow the cord was compromised, kinked or squeezed so oxygen couldn't get through to her.

I showered and got dressed. Pat came back and helped me gather my things, hurrying me along so we wouldn't be charged for another full day. A nurse wheeled me out in a wheelchair. It was sunny but chilly outside. We drove to the mortuary and picked up Clara Marie's body in a box. It felt strange holding the cardboard box, knowing I could no longer hold the baby inside.

The mortician showed us some caskets. I couldn't stand up very long and felt like I was going to pass out. They said they wouldn't be able to embalm her because she'd never breathed outside the womb, but that was okay because I didn't feel capable of viewing her again—I'd already said my good-byes. (They didn't embalm her but did do something to her so that we could have a family viewing.)

When I came home, JoRene had cleaned the house top to bottom. But she hadn't put away the baby things. It was difficult for me to do, but in the process I was able to experience grief and allow it to be part of me for a while. Caree (six) came in when I first came home and we cried and cried together. Kirt (four) and Keith (two) seemed oblivious to it all. I found Camille (eight) crying on her bed. I held her and we cried some more.

January 30

Kim and Kirt were allowed to dig Clara Marie's grave today. A city official suggested that we dig it ourselves so that Kim could be a part of things. It was something he could do for his daughter.

January 31

We had the graveside services today. My mom, Kim's parents, and most of his brothers and sisters came. Pat came. I had a pretty little dress I wanted to dress her in, one that was just her size. Pam brought a beautiful bonnet, and JoRene embroidered it to match the dress. Mom bought her some tights and some little booties. We wrapped her in a pretty white shawl. Kim bought her a little turquoise bracelet.

We had a family viewing and prayer. Camille didn't want to touch her, but I encouraged her by telling her how holding the baby helped me to get over the hurt. Kirt seemed extremely interested and kept touching her head where the bones were separating on the skull. Keith kept saying, "Ours baby's dead." Caree cried and cried and desperately wanted to touch her, almost out of curiosity. It bothered Caree that Clara Marie's lips and all around her mouth were wrinkled and that soon all of her body would look ugly. I tried to explain that the next time we see her she will be beautiful again.

The coffin looked beautiful with all the flowers over it. Harvey spoke and there was a song. They wanted to lower her into the ground while we were there but I decided I didn't want to watch so Pat and I went for a walk around the cemetery while Kim and the kids watched the casket being lowered.

March 1984

I have good days and bad days. I had the opportunity of helping a friend who had a stillborn baby just ten days after I did. It was her first baby and she hadn't been married long, about a year. She was having a hard time and was numb. Hearing of her experience in the hospital—she had to have pitocin to start her labor, she was heavily sedated, and she didn't even get to hold her baby—made me appreciate the way everyone handled my care and healing. I'm grateful the birth happened where it did, with Pat helping and guiding, with Dr.

Cullum and the nurses so understanding and capable, with JoRene near and Mom able to come so soon afterwards. The Lord has been watchful over me. He has made it possible for me to heal. I feel His gentle arms around me. There have been times when I can actually physically feel the healing happening.

January 28, 1985

I gave birth to a beautiful baby girl one year to the day after we lost our sweet Clara Marie. When I found out I would be giving birth around the same time—one year later—I prayed that it wouldn't be on the same day. When I went into labor on the 28th it felt like a cruel joke. How could I possibly do this again? But once again I allowed the healing to happen. I allowed myself to be open to life. I trusted that whatever happened would be for my good. When I first held my baby she looked at me as if she had an understanding of all that had gone on. For hours her wise look entranced me. We named her Crystal.

Chapter Six

CLIMBING JACOB'S LADDER
by Christie Frandsen

> AND [JACOB] DREAMED, AND BEHOLD A LADDER SET UP ON THE EARTH AND THE TOP OF IT REACHED TO HEAVEN: AND BEHOLD THE ANGELS OF GOD ASCENDING AND DESCENDING ON IT. . . . AND JACOB AWAKED OUT OF HIS SLEEP, AND HE SAID, SURELY THE LORD IS IN THIS PLACE; AND I KNEW IT NOT. AND HE WAS AFRAID, AND SAID, HOW DREADFUL IS THIS PLACE! THIS IS NONE OTHER BUT THE HOUSE OF GOD, AND THIS IS THE GATE OF HEAVEN.
>
> —GENESIS 28:12,16–17

Jacob's first headache came on Halloween the year he was three. In the midst of the exuberant chaos generated in getting seven young children transformed into gypsies and cowboys, I hadn't noticed how quiet Jacob was that afternoon. Usually cheerfully rambunctious, he and his twin sister, Rachel, had been looking forward to their first real Halloween of trick-or-treating with the big kids and Daddy. Rachel was going as a princess; Jacob was to be a fireman, complete with a short length of hose he had discovered with delight in the garden shed. But now, just an hour before the Primary costume parade, his excited anticipation had disappeared, swallowed up by the pain that wracked his little blond head. I couldn't remember ever having a three-year-old complain of a headache before—tummy aches and "owies" of various sorts on every other part of the body, yes.

Christie Frandsen *is a homemaker, volunteer Institute teacher, and freelance writer from La Canada, California. She and her husband, Russ, are the parents of eleven children. She is currently Young Women president in her ward and teaches Institute at Glendale Community College and USC.*

But never a headache. I pushed the nagging concern to the back of my mind as I hurriedly readied other children for the big night. For the first time in her life, Rachel went off without Jacob by her side. She took along an extra jack-o-lantern bucket to bring home some candy for her twin. Jacob stayed home that evening with eight-month-old Benjamin and me, quietly resting in the darkness of the family room, a cool cloth on his forehead to help ease the pain. The fireman's costume lay untouched in the bottom of the dress-up trunk. He never went trick-or-treating—not that night, not ever.

The headaches continued with increasing frequency and intensity during the next two and a half months. The pediatrician was puzzled, but didn't seem overly concerned. When I asked if he thought a CAT scan should be done, he assured me that such extreme measures were absolutely uncalled for at this point. I felt I had no justification for questioning the doctor's judgment, and so I did nothing but try the best I could to help Jacob deal with the pain. His pain became the newest and most demanding member of our family. It was relentlessly unpredictable as it came and went, victimizing the entire family. Weekend outings were abruptly cut short; half-filled grocery carts were left abandoned at the market; we rushed Jacob home in the middle of music recitals and school programs; the frustration and anxiety mounted. I look back now and realize that none of us guessed the extent of Jacob's suffering.

It's astonishing how naturally we can accommodate even the most drastic change when it comes slowly and insidiously. I knew Jacob wasn't looking very well, but it took my mother's visit in January to open my eyes to the seriousness of his condition. To her, the contrast between the robust, sturdy little boy she had seen in the summer and this pale, listless child with haunting dark circles under his eyes was dramatic and frightening. At her insistence, we called a pediatric neurologist. The first available appointment was nearly a month away, but as I described Jacob's symptoms—headaches, lethargy, irritability, vomiting—the receptionist's tone changed abruptly and she said without hesitation, "We'll squeeze him in today." The chill of fear tucked into that far corner of my mind began to spread.

Thirty minutes later I sat in the doctor's office, cradling Jacob in my arms as I answered endless questions regarding his medical history and tried to calm him during the doctor's examination. Jacob was frightened and tense. So was I. Still, I clung fiercely to the determined faith that any moment now the doctor would tell me exactly what was wrong with my child, prescribe a simple medication, and we could resume a normal life. That delusion shattered into a thousand piercing shards as I saw what the doctor was writing on Jacob's chart: *preliminary diagnosis—brain tumor*.

My husband's patriarchal blessing contains a phrase that had puzzled him for years: "Be not discouraged when the way seems dark, for as a noble son in Israel you will be tried and tested." In that sunlit office, my face buried in Jacob's tousled baby-soft hair, I heard the Spirit clearly whisper in my mind, "The dark days are here."

After nearly a month of invasive and traumatic diagnostic tests, the doctors determined that Jacob had a rare form of cancer called astrocytoma. The primary tumor was on his spinal cord—spreading its hideous tentacles around the cord, up through the brain stem, and into the brain. The cancer had clogged the normal flow of fluid between the spinal column and the brain, causing a buildup of pressure on the brain and the excruciating headaches. In a delicate and extremely dangerous eight-hour surgery, the doctors took as much of the tumor as they could safely remove and inserted a shunt under Jacob's skin from his head to his abdomen to drain the accumulating fluid. Jacob felt better than he had for months. The battle had begun.

Cancer is an ugly word. It was several weeks before I could say it out loud when concerned friends asked what was happening. "Jacob has a tumor," or even, "Jacob has a rare condition called astrocytoma"—anything was better than, "Jacob has cancer." It is terrible enough that cancer viciously attacks older people who have the strength to fight back and the wisdom to understand why these things sometimes happen. But when it strikes at our children, our babies, so completely innocent and vulnerable with their whole lives ahead of them, it is devastating beyond words. I remember eleven-year-old Gabrielle sobbing one night, "Why did this have to happen to Jacob? It isn't fair!" All I could say was, "There's nothing fair about cancer and no one on this earth has any answers. Let's not think about all the whys right now. Let's just do everything we can to make Jacob better." Why is it that all the important questions have no answers?

We were astonished to discover an entire hospital ward full of "Cancer Kids" dealing heroically with burdens their small bodies should never have had to bear. That first time we stepped onto the floor of 4-West at Children's Hospital of Los Angeles, I looked around and thought, "We don't belong here; Jacob will never be like these other children; he will never lose his hair; he will never cruise through the halls pushing an IV pole around as naturally as if it were another appendage; he will never be that painfully thin. This isn't going to happen to my little boy." I resisted getting to know the other mothers who seemed eager to welcome a new member into this bizarre club. But within a very few weeks I felt more at home on 4-West than I did in my ward. There is a spontaneous and powerful camaraderie that comes with fighting a common enemy. Jacob did, indeed, begin to look just like all of his newfound friends, bald head and all.

My oldest daughter Rosalynde, age thirteen, worried about his hair falling out. She worried that children would tease Jacob, that we would be even more conspicuous than we already were. She had nightmares of going to the grocery store and hearing total strangers whisper, "There's that poor family who has the little boy with cancer. Aren't they pitiful?"

Her nightmare became reality. Jacob's bald head did prompt many comments from others—some rude, some curious and thoughtless, some compassionate. But as it turned out, we ceased caring what anyone else thought of our family. We ceased caring about many things that had previously seemed important—things like getting new furniture and keeping an immaculate yard, and even things like whether Jacob's cancer treatment might slow him down developmentally. Everything soon faded into oblivion in the face of the only issue that really mattered—survival. Cancer is a powerful reality check.

From the very beginning my husband and I told the doctors we wanted to know everything concerning Jacob's cancer and treatment options. We felt that knowledge was power and we wanted to be involved in the decisions that would so greatly affect our lives. The doctors took us at our word and were honest and open with us, giving us resources to learn all there was to know about this rare cancer that Jacob had. The truth was brutal. There were no known ten-year survivors of Jacob's cancer. Still, new drugs were being developed all the time and experimental treatments were promising better results. They gave us a ten percent chance. That was enough for hope to take root.

Jacob's treatment involved five days of hospitalization for intravenous chemotherapy followed by two weeks at home to rest and recover strength. He would have ten or twelve "rounds" of chemo, and then, hopefully, we would be finished. That didn't sound too bad; we could handle that. We didn't ask the obvious "What if?" We didn't look that far ahead. "Just get through one day at a time," was the advice I had been given by the veteran mothers on 4-West.

I soon learned that the theory of chemotherapy bears little resemblance to its reality. We never did settle into any sort of predictable routine during Jacob's illness. His was a difficult case from the beginning and continued to be full of unexpected twists and turns—*complications*, they were called on 4-West. And they did make life complicated for us. The children got accustomed to arriving home to find a note on the kitchen table: "Jacob got a nosebleed. We're in the hospital for a transfusion. Rachel and Benjamin are at Jessica's. Fix macaroni and cheese for dinner. Get your homework and practicing done. Don't forget to brush your teeth and say your prayers. I love you!" Nosebleeds, fevers, infections, and vomiting were all potentially life-threatening for Jacob with his suppressed immune system and damaged blood supply. We were in and out of the hospital constantly. It was hard on the children and hard on me. I was forced to wean my baby and had to rely on the kindness of dear friends to take my little ones at a moment's notice. We had always been among the givers in our ward and community, but now suddenly we were everyone's compassionate service project. We struggled mightily to maintain as much self-sufficiency as we could. My big girls became very practiced at fixing dinner and supervising homework and bedtime. But in the end we had to learn the difficult lesson of receiving graciously. It was a humbling time for our family.

In the midst of my preoccupation with Jacob's needs I tried the best I could not to forget that I had six other children who also needed me. We managed, barely, to keep up with school projects, music lessons, Scouting activities, and even had a few picnics in the park, although neither the quality nor the quantity of my time was adequate. The children were remarkably resilient and understanding. I believe they all realized they were sacrificing for Jacob and were blessed for it. Along with normal life, there were milestones that deserved celebrating. Rosalynde graduated from junior high school; Gabrielle won the sixth grade speech contest; Brigham was baptized in our backyard swimming pool; and Jacob and Rachel went off to their first day of preschool. Life went marching inexorably on, though there were many times when I desperately wanted to call a time-out. If I had had the power I would have put everything on hold and focused exclusively on Jacob. And, tragically, Jacob would have missed out on all the good that life would ever offer him. These times together—the special and the ordinary—were challenging, but especially poignant. We took lots of pictures, we bought a video camera, we made tape recordings. In the back of our minds was the ever-present but unspoken thought that we might never be together like this again.

Yet we were optimistic. By the end of the summer the tumors were shrinking measurably and Jacob was feeling quite well in spite of his steady weight loss. Our family project that summer was feeding Jacob. He got anything his heart desired, anytime, anywhere. The older girls were unfailingly attentive, even indulgent. I remember worrying that Jacob would be insufferably spoiled by the time he was better, but instead he grew sweeter and more appreciative and loving as time passed. As the circle of Jacob's life drew smaller the love he felt and gave seemed to expand ever greater.

It was during these summer months that I noticed a rivalry developing among my three oldest daughters concerning Jacob. Each was wanting desperately to be Jacob's favorite sister—the one he called for when he was sick, the one who could best comfort him, the one who could coax him into eating. I tried to convince them that there was enough love to go around, that in a family there are no contests for love. We needed to work together—they needed to be each other's best friends. I'm not sure my lectures helped. In the end I didn't have the energy to deal with the complex emotional needs of my healthy children. I found myself echoing Scarlett O'Hara's familiar refrain, "I'll think about it tomorrow."

Our optimism faded with the passing of summer. I was the first to notice the subtle changes in Jacob's condition. Even before there was any measurable difference to alert the doctors, I knew the chemotherapy was no longer working. His fatigue and irritability increased, the dark circles under his eyes returned, and his hair started growing back—not wispy blond anymore, but thick, dark, and wavy. The girls were thrilled about Jacob's "new look," and I didn't burden them with my foreboding. But it didn't take long for Rosalynde to start figuring things out. One night she confronted me. "If Jacob's hair is growing back, does that mean the cancer is too?" I didn't know what to answer. I said something vague like, "Oh, there's nothing to worry about," but she looked unconvinced. She was too smart to be fooled.

We were told in January that Jacob had "failed" chemotherapy. That's an odd expression. It seems to me that chemotherapy failed Jacob. Not only did it fail to cure his cancer, it left his body decimated by its powerful toxins. It seemed as if it destroyed almost everything except the cancer. His kidneys were damaged, his hearing impaired, his immune system and blood chemistry were compromised. Yet the cancer was growing faster than ever. There were a few other experimental treatments that we could have tried, but they would have required extensive hospitalization and additional trauma for Jacob. After fasting and prayer, we decided that Jacob had been through enough. We decided to bring him home to stay for as long as he had left. The doctors had no idea how long that might be—a few weeks, maybe a few months. We asked how we would know when death was imminent and were told, "You'll know."

Telling the children was heart-wrenchingly difficult. Telling Jacob was even harder. How do you tell a child, not yet five, that he is going to die? What words are there to explain to one so young why the doctors and the medicine and the blessings and the faith were not sufficient to bring the miracle he believed would come? As I told him what heaven would be like, I found my faith shaken to the core. Was I really so sure? What if I was wrong? I had failed Jacob in life, what if I was also failing him in death—holding out false promises and creating pipe dreams? How could I say I knew these things were true? In the end it was Jacob's faith and trusting acceptance that sustained me. His only fear was being alone. I promised him with as much confidence as my frayed testimony could muster that he would never be alone, not for one instant. And I am certain now that he was not.

Jacob died on May 2. Gathered around him were Rosalynde, Gabrielle, my mother, my husband, and me. And others too. Angels were waiting there for him on the other side. Though I didn't see them, I know they were there. He was never alone. He had lingered longer than anyone thought possible. He was emaciated, could no longer talk, probably could not hear or see much at the end, but he could love. I am convinced that he sensed our struggle against his death and clung to life for the sake of his family, waiting patiently until we were ready to let him go. I hope with all my heart that we were able to keep him relatively pain-free, though I know his last weeks were far from comfortable. As I watched him slip slowly away, I wondered if I could die with such courage and grace as Jacob. The second hardest thing I have ever done in my life was to let go of the hope that Jacob would live, that our ram in the thicket would miraculously appear. Sometimes even now I cannot believe I had the strength to offer that prayer of relinquishment: "Release him from his suffering, Father. Take him back home with You."

But that was not the hardest part. The hardest thing I have ever done was to go on living without him. He had been the center of my life for eighteen months of intense emotion and effort. And now, after one last faint beating of his valiant heart, he was gone. All of those well-meaning people who told me the hardest part would be having to watch him die were so very wrong.

Our family was consumed with grief. It filled every crevice and crack in our home, poured out of the doors and windows into our yard, and trailed behind us as we went to church and school and pretended to be living. And much like Jacob's cancer, it seemed to grow and gather strength daily during that first year without him, enveloping every member of our family with its piercing influence. Benjamin was only two years old, but he felt its grip. Abraham Jacob, born exactly three months to the day before his big brother Jacob died, was nursed with grief-laced mother's milk. Rosalynde and Gabrielle, ages fourteen and twelve, grieved more openly, yet each so differently from the other. Naomi and Brigham, ages ten and eight, seemed outwardly to be the least affected, but they held unexpressed emotions that needed careful release. And then there was Rachel, who had lost her twin brother. Her whole sense of identity was wrenched apart. That is not easily or quickly reconstructed. We went to the cemetery every Sunday after church to talk about Jacob and sing his favorite songs and cry. There were many who raised their eyebrows and gently suggested that we needed to "move on." But we didn't want to. Moving on would mean leaving Jacob behind, and we just couldn't. Not yet, maybe not ever.

I read several helpful books on the grieving process for adults, but there was nothing written to help me guide my children through their grief. I was in no position to rescue my children, emotionally and physically drained as I was. Yet, whether through instincts or inspiration, I feel we were led to do some things that worked for our family. I can also see clearly now some things we didn't do that would have eased the way for our children. Nine years later, having gone through the process again with the death of a premature son, Isaac, nearly two years ago, I feel our experience might be of some value to other families. I share these experiences, not by way of prescription, but in the spirit of deepest compassion, knowing that everyone's grief is most intensely personal and unique and knowing that there is only one true source of comfort and that is the Comforter himself.

When someone in the family dies, children are left with memories—and questions. Many times the questions are never asked, but haunt their minds and sometimes erode their faith until they find answers that make sense to them. This can be a long and painful process which may take years to resolve peacefully. Often the questions need to be asked again and again as the child matures and readdresses the loss of that loved one. Sometimes emotional and spiritual scars remain throughout life. No one is ever the same after an encounter with death. But I believe with wise and patient guidance, answers and peace can be found that will leave children stronger emotionally and spiritually.

It is critical to keep in mind the child's age when helping someone find answers to the questions that come with a death. A teenager will have a very different set of concerns than a young child. That became obvious to me as I tried to help my six children who were ages fourteen to newborn. The age categories that I will use are: Teenagers (age eleven and older), Elementary School Children (ages seven–ten), Young Children (ages three–six), and Babies (age two and younger). Another crucial factor is the relationship to the loved one who died. Dealing with the death of a grandparent is far different from dealing with the death of a parent, and different still from dealing with the death of a sibling. I can only comment on sibling grief. With this, it is important to consider the position in the family and the nature of the relationship. Was this a younger or older sibling? Was it the sibling closest in age? How close was the emotional connection between the children? Was there any forewarning or preparation for the death, or did it come without warning? Did the children get a chance to say good-bye and resolve any conflicts they may have had? All of these factors would greatly affect a child's grief response. The best we can do is make some general observations.

TEENAGERS

The teenage years are already a time of highly charged emotion and conflict. Dealing with death, especially an unexpected or untimely death, makes the emotions all the more intense and overpowering. Teenagers often experience deep anger and bitter resentment that can threaten their basic religious faith. "Why weren't my prayers answered?" "Doesn't God care about me?" "What kind of God would let my little brother die of cancer?" Teenagers do not want pat answers and trite cliches, and yet they lack the broad spiritual experience and knowledge to really understand these complex issues. They vacillate between being young adults grappling with the weighty matters of God's nature and acting young, immature, and self-centered, asking things like "Would my parents miss me as much?" "When will my mother quit being so sad all the time so I can invite my friends over?"

Teenagers tend to be judgmental and can be critical of the grief responses of their parents or siblings. "My sister obviously didn't love Jacob as much as I did or she wouldn't be going to that party with her friends." "Why doesn't my father ever cry when he talks about Jacob?" They don't realize that there is more than one right way to grieve.

For some teenagers these painful emotions and inner conflicts may be more than they can handle—they turn away from it, walling off the parts of their hearts that hurt too much to bear. They refuse to talk about it and do everything they can to keep from feeling the pain. These children are especially vulnerable and need careful and wise monitoring and many non-threatening opportunities to open up, whether verbally or through writing or art. Sometimes a close family friend or a trusted teacher is more effective than a parent in dealing with these young people.

With good communication, patience, and lots of prayer, most teenagers process their grief in healthy ways. But others need professional help. If a teenager experiences a personality change or intense debilitating sorrow that persists for more than six months, make an appointment with a skilled grief counselor.

My two oldest daughters, Rosalynde and Gabrielle, are very different in personality and grieved very differently. Rosalynde is emotionally open and verbally expressive. Gabrielle is more closed and private, sullenly silent when she's upset. Rosalynde is cheerful and happy; Gabrielle is moody. As the oldest, they carried a huge burden during Jacob's illness and sacrificed their carefree junior high years to the family crisis. Their sacrifice for Jacob began even before he got sick. They were my extra pair of arms during the twins' early years. That level of sacrifice created an unusually deep bond of love between the girls and Jacob and, of course, an equally deep grief at his death. I let them stay home from school for several days after his death and funeral, but the time came when they had to return. It was difficult knowing how to relate to friends and teachers, some of whom didn't know anything about Jacob, most of whom were very uncomfortable with the whole situation. It was awkward and painful, yet had to be faced. Rosalynde learned that honest communication works well in easing others' discomfort in the presence of a grieving friend. Gabrielle learned that friends drift away when you keep your heart from them. They both learned that not everyone knows how to console, that tactless comments can hurt deeply, and that friends seem to forget all about what happened sooner than you wish they would. These are hard lessons in reality for young girls. Rosalynde came home many days and wept, while Gabrielle withdrew silently into her room.

Then there was the day when Rosalynde came home from school and realized with a start that she had not thought about Jacob all day—life had pulled her from her consuming grief and swept her along in its current. And then Rosalynde really wept. Her memories and her grief were all that she had left of Jacob. If she let go of the grief, even for a moment, she feared she would lose Jacob and betray her love for him. It was a long time before she was able to understand that grief and love are not always synonymous. Eventually the raw wound of grief healed and the deep love and sweet memories remained. Rosalynde expresses her feelings verbally and also in writing. A gifted writer, she kept a journal throughout Jacob's illness which was an invaluable emotional outlet for her. She wrote poetry and essays as her way of processing her feelings, preserving her memories, and also paying tribute to her brother. Jacob is a continual presence in her life and will be forever.

Gabrielle was more deeply scarred from Jacob's death. When she closed the door to her room and shut out the rest of the family, she closed herself off from solace and reassurance—and answers. She had some deep theological questions that needed answers, but had no way of finding those answers on her own. Seminary, Sunday School, and family home evening gave her no satisfying answers. Since she never asked me anything directly, I didn't realize how dangerously she was floundering. There were signs that I should have recognized—she lost connection with her Church friends, read during sacrament meeting, immersed herself in academics, and became deeply interested in the Ayn Rand philosophy of moral objectivism. She was lonely and unhappy, but I didn't realize what was the cause of her struggling. In retrospect I should never have allowed her to isolate herself so much from family and Church. I should have spent much more time talking with her, giving her opportunities to open up and explore her deepest fears and doubts. Whenever she began to talk of doubts, I expressed such alarm over her feelings that she didn't dare continue. So she stopped talking and almost stopped believing. By the time I realized what was happening to Gabrielle, it was too late for me to repair the damage. She was off to college and all I could do was pray with all the energy of my heart for a miracle to rescue Gabrielle and restore her faith. That miracle came, as so many do, in the form of unconditional love. She is married now and happier than she has been in years. She still has a hard time trusting and opening up emotionally, she still struggles with making friends, but she is working on these issues. Some scars take a lifetime to fade.

One thing we did right with Gabrielle was to encourage her to learn all she could about Jacob's illness. Knowledge is power; knowledge helps restore order in a child's world thrown into chaos; knowledge can bring peace. At the suggestion of a wise teacher, Gabrielle did a study of astrocytoma for a school science project. After hours of research and interviewing Jacob's doctors, she put together an impressive presentation of cancer and the scientific principles behind chemotherapy. But even more remarkable and moving was the series of pictures she displayed showing the impact this illness had on Jacob and our family. The throngs of people who looked at Gabrielle's display moved on a little quieter, more reflective, and touched by the life of this little boy. For Gabrielle it was a triumph she desperately needed.

Elementary School Children

These are the years in children's lives when they should be happy and carefree and totally absorbed in all the busy activities of learning and growing. Well-adjusted children of this age hardly know what sorrow feels like. The process of grieving is absolutely foreign to their cheerful and ebullient natures. They have only a superficial understanding of the cycles of life and death and of the plan of salvation. So when death occurs the biggest challenge can often be to help them to feel grief. The questions they ask are, "When will our life ever get back to normal?" "Is it OK to laugh?" "Is there something wrong with me if I don't feel sad at the cemetery?" Life is too exciting and fast-paced for these children to waste much time feeling bad, yet it is important for them to feel appropriate sorrow, or they might grow up with a haunting sense of guilt that they didn't love their brother enough.

For children this age it helps to spend time remembering their loved one by looking at photo albums or videotapes, sharing memories and anecdotes, and encouraging the child to write the memories in a journal so that when he grows up, he has this personal record as evidence of his love. My children assembled a memory book for Jacob that has become a treasure in our home, especially for our younger children who never knew Jacob.

As we spent time sharing our memories I became aware that memories of children are often distorted or incomplete (of course, sometimes adult memories are too), leaving them with a false perception of what really happened. With time these false memories become their reality, a false reality that could wound children emotionally or spiritually. It's important to clarify these misconceptions before they become entrenched and damaging. This is another powerful argument for taking time to remember and rehearse the stories of our past, as Moses, Nephi, Jacob, and so many other prophets admonished their people to do. (See the first chapters of the Book of Mormon for a sobering illustration of the spiritual and emotional ruin that can come to a family torn apart by false perceptions.)

Our regular visits to the cemetery gave us dedicated time for remembering and feeling. For the first year we went every Sunday, but the need gradually diminished. Now we go several times a year. These visits are not mandatory, and there have been times when someone hasn't wanted to go. There is never any coercion and usually everyone is happy to come along. A ritual has developed that, I hope, satisfies everyone's needs. We clean and polish the grave marker, trim the grass and arrange fresh flowers, then we sing some of Jacob's favorite songs, spend a few minutes reminiscing, and leave before it gets tedious for anyone. On Christmas every year we each send up a helium balloon with our Christmas promises attached. (I realize it is not exactly ecologically correct to send off helium balloons, but we only do it once a year.) We try to keep the mood reflective but not somber. When the little boys get rowdy and begin rolling down the hill, as they invariably do, we remind ourselves that Jacob himself would be doing that were he with us. Now that my older daughters are marrying and bringing new members into our family, this ritual is even more important, I believe. To truly know and understand our family it is essential to know about Jacob and Isaac and the continuing role they play in our lives.

Elementary school children are not always superficial, of course. Their feelings can sometimes be overpowering. Children this age are more likely to feel fear, rather than the anger of the teenager. They can experience deep fears that they are often unable to articulate. "Why didn't God answer my prayers?" "What happens when you die?" Some of their fears are irrational, but very real to them: "Was it my fault that Jacob died?" "Will I die young too?" This is an opportunity to teach and reassure, even if the questions go unasked. I found that when I gently probed, the questions and concerns and feelings came pouring out and we could share a precious teaching moment. For many children, sitting face to face on the couch is too formal and awkward. Driving in the car to piano lessons or taking a walk around the block at twilight are better settings for these tender discussions. I wish I had done this more with Naomi and Brigham. I'm afraid I was too preoccupied with the needs of the little ones and the older ones—I was too busy and too tired to search after unexpressed needs. I remember seeing Brigham weep for his little brothers only three times, yet I know his feelings are deep and sometimes troubled. These middle children are not always as unaffected as they appear.

YOUNG CHILDREN

The death of a twin is probably rare—I hope it is. In many ways, Rachel experienced the most profound loss of all, and at an age when she was hardly able to comprehend it. For young children the finality of death is almost impossible to understand. Fantasy and reality are still interwoven in their minds. Fairy tales and dragons and leprechauns and Santa Claus are as real as their family. Death has no place in those fantasies. We haven't had a television in our home, but a thoughtful friend brought one over during those last difficult weeks of Jacob's life and Rachel began watching videos. It kept her entertained and distracted from the heavy sorrow in our home. Her favorite was *Sleeping Beauty*. She watched it over and over again. I paid no attention to her obsessive viewing until one day when I caught sight of Rachel bending over her sleeping twin brother and gently kissing him on the lips. And then I knew I had to do more to help Rachel understand the reality of death. For her, life without Jacob was inconceivable. She had never been without him. We made special arrangements with the hospital to allow Rachel to spend many hours with Jacob while he was hospitalized. She had been his main support, and he was hers. I had encouraged this closeness and had done everything I could to give them opportunities to be together. But now I had to somehow prepare Rachel to find a life, an identity, without Jacob.

We were blessed to have a nurse whose twin brother had died of leukemia when she was young. She gave us valuable insight and counsel. After the death of her brother her parents were so grief stricken that they removed every picture of her brother from the house, which was also every picture of her. Their inability to keep him as a presence in their family was emotionally devastating for her; they robbed her of all of her happy childhood memories. We vowed not to do that to Rachel. Our walls are covered with pictures of Rachel and Jacob. And yet it was important for us to help Rachel know that she exists independent of Jacob as well. We value her for her own intrinsic worth, not only because she is Jacob's twin. There is a tendency in a family to "deify" the child who has died. Gradually the child takes on legendary dimensions and no one remembers that he ever did anything wrong in his life. And the child who is left wonders how she can ever measure up and begins to think that is why she had to stay behind. The burden of a perfect twin, or perfect sibling, is too heavy for any child to bear. We have tried not to idealize Jacob in our family stories, all the while preserving the memories of his sweet purity that can help to inspire us all.

Jealousy of the ill child, who is getting all the attention, or a deep resentment of the child who died and took away all the family happiness may also develop. Most children, even young children, understand that these feelings are not acceptable, so when they come, they experience feelings of guilt that complicate things even further. "I must be a terrible person for being jealous of my brother." Of course, young children are not usually able to articulate these feelings, but they certainly feel them and often their behavior reflects their conflicted emotions. Parents can help to alleviate these feelings very simply—by giving enough attention to the young child. We were careful to make sure that Rachel got occasional presents, along with Jacob. When my mother came to stay with us the last weeks of Jacob's life, she took Rachel under her wing. They were inseparable, and Rachel was appropriately "spoiled" by Grandma's treats. It worked miracles in her life.

A common grief response for a young child is regression. I was astonished to see my mature five-year-old revert to baby talk and silly flirtations with my husband every evening when he arrived home from work. She insisted on climbing on him and playing baby games. She was acting like a three-year-old. It was almost as if she had to go back and grow up all over again, this time without Jacob, as she struggled to rebuild her identity. She began to stutter and she did not want to talk about Jacob. She still does not, and yet she is the first one to remind us that it has been a long time since we visited the cemetery.

Rachel writes poetry that is intense and yearning and lonely. She is a solitary person. When Isaac died two years ago, Rachel was tense and steely at the cemetery, clenching her jaws tight and turning away from the circle of our grieving family. I long to talk to her of Jacob and her feelings, but she is not ready yet. I wonder what she might have been like had Jacob lived. I wonder what their relationship would have been like. Every time Rachel reaches a milestone, we are reminded painfully of our loss as we celebrate with her. His shadow will remain with her forever.

For young children, a death in the family is always a double loss—not only did they lose a sibling, but also a happy, functioning parent. For several years I was only going through the motions of mothering, my heart was not in it. I remember seeing a plaque on the wall in a friend's kitchen that read: "When Mama's not happy, ain't nobody happy." My children can all vouch for the truthfulness of that sentiment. After I emerged from the darkest months of grieving, it seemed I forgot how to be happy. Even now, nine years later, I have to remind myself to lighten up and have fun with my children. My young children have been raised in a home that is too intense, where curtains are kept drawn, where chores and practicing and homework occupy our time, and life is serious business.

Yet there is hope, and it has come in the form of Christian and Eva, my two youngest, who were born after Jacob died. Every morning Christian jumps from his bed and proceeds to pull open all the curtains upstairs, letting the sunlight come flooding into dark corners where deep sorrow still lurks. He sings and dances and plays Indians with Eva and reminds me that "Man is that he might have joy." I look at Christian and remember that this is what Jacob was like before he got sick. Some of those long-forgotten feelings of lighthearted, innocent delight come back and I see glimpses of myself as I was before the weight of cancer and death and grief changed me.

Babies

When Jacob died, I had two babies—Benjamin was two years old and Abraham Jacob was three months old. Though they have no conscious memory of this time, they were affected by the general atmosphere of our home and especially by my depressed spirit. During the course of Jacob's illness, I had to leave Benjamin far more often than I had ever left a baby. I agonized over this, yet there was no choice, and Benjamin certainly received loving care from the women who tended him. As it turned out, Benjamin wasn't the most affected by the separation—I was. I learned firsthand that maternal bonding is not an automatic response. It comes as a result of spending time with that child. I was spending far more time with Jacob than I was with Benjamin, and so my emotional ties to Jacob were stronger than they were with Benjamin. When Jacob died, I had some serious make-up work to do with Benjamin. It was frightening for me to come face to face with my own emotional deficiencies as a mother. And yet I am grateful that I recognized the problem in time to do something about it. In those first months after Jacob died, I made a conscious effort to reforge the bonds of love with my energetic, bright little boy. I learned that time does heal many wounds and that toddlers are remarkably resilient and forgiving. Benjamin and I are very close today. In many ways, he is the most like me of all my children—very focused, a little too intense, subject to emotional meltdowns occasionally. Sometimes I remind Benjamin that he paid a dear price for Jacob's well-being, and I believe it makes him feel honored to have been a part of the family sacrifice.

The last thing I thought I needed in the middle of Jacob's illness was a new baby. I was overwhelmed with anxiety when I discovered I was pregnant. How in the world would I be able to manage? Didn't Heavenly Father know my limitations? Through the loud murmurings of my spirit I heard the still small voice assure me that Heavenly Father did in fact know exactly what He was doing and that I would understand in due time. We knew a month before Abraham was born that Jacob would die, and then I understood the Lord's timing. It is no overstatement to say that this small, unanticipated baby Abraham kept me from sinking into the depths of despair those first months after Jacob died. Many times I felt that my family would be better off without me—all except Abraham, who needed me to nurse him and love him. And how I needed him. He filled my arms when my heart was empty. He gave me love when I didn't deserve any. He turned my mind to the future when I would have languished in the past. Abraham's role in the grieving process of our family was inestimable. He remains today a loving and affectionate child who can read my moods better than anyone else in the family.

FUNERALS

So many decisions need to be made at the death of a family member, among them the details of the funeral. This has been an issue of great concern for many families as they struggled to decide which children should go to the funeral, which should stay home, and which, if any, should be allowed to view the open casket. I will simply share what our family did. All of our children, except Benjamin and Abraham, attended Jacob's funeral, as well as the viewing that was held for close family friends prior to the funeral. I do not believe it was traumatic in any way. On the contrary I believe it was an important time of closure for the children. They needed to see that, in fact, Jacob's living spirit was not being buried, only the shell of his body. They each had a chance to see his face one last time and to whisper one last good-bye. The funeral was tender and emotional, but not excessively so. It was good for the children to see the outpouring of love and support from our ward and community and to realize how many people cared. My one regret is that I did not have my children participate in the funeral. It never occurred to me how much it might mean to them to have the chance to pay a public tribute to their brother. The four oldest wrote poems that we printed and gave to those attending the funeral. But I wish I had had them sing a song in the program. It would have been difficult, but the memory would have been sweet and lingering.

A Retrospective

Nine years have passed since Jacob's death. Our family was changed by that experience. Are we better, stronger, more compassionate, more united because of his death? I do not know. I'm sure that is what is supposed to happen when an LDS family survives the death of a loved one, but honestly, I don't know if we are a better family. Many times I am certain that I am not better. I believe I was at my best during Jacob's illness. I think I really rose to the occasion and the incredible demands of those months—or, more likely, I was carried through it by the Lord. But grief changed me, and I'm not sure I'm as nice a person as I once was in my days of innocence. I have greater hope for my children. I see them growing up strong and wonderful, with a focus and sense of responsibility that many young people lack. We have our eyes fixed on the celestial kingdom in our family. It is our only hope for a first-time family gathering. Never have I had all of my children together at the same time. We yearn for that possibility and I believe it is a source of spiritual motivation for all of us.

Yet scars remain—and ephemeral glimpses of our two boys, one who would be tall and athletic, playing soccer in the backyard, running stride for stride with his twin sister, the other a sixteen-month-old crawling into cupboards and bringing the pure delight only a baby can bring into a home. Couldn't our family have been as good and strong and focused on eternal pursuits with our two boys here? Was there truly no other way?

The scars haunt me even more because I feel responsible for them. If I had only been wiser, less preoccupied with my own loss, more spiritually tuned to the needs of my children—if only I had talked with them more, prayed with them more, helped them to reach through and beyond the pain, they would have done better. But I didn't. And so now I pray daily that the healing powers of the Atonement will make them whole again. I pray with all my heart that my mistakes will not be answered upon the heads of my children. I pray that, as they turn to Him, He will turn ashes to beauty in their lives.

As a family we have sensed the angels ascending and descending on Jacob's ladder. Heaven is not as far away as it sometimes feels. I would agree with Jacob of old that it is sometimes a dreadful sight. We have begun that steep ascent, many rungs below Jacob and Isaac. Yet we can see them in the mists above, beckoning us to follow and not fear. And if we look steadily above, we can, every now and again, catch a glint from the gates of heaven.

WHEN I WAS ELEVEN
by Naomi Frandsen

When I was eleven my little brother Jacob died of cancer. A couple of months later a group of child psychologists from Children's Hospital came to administer a written test to Rosalynde, Gabrielle, Brigham, and me. We were the children "dealing" with Jacob's death, and I guess they were curious to see if we were doing it right. That afternoon was warm, I remember, and as I knelt up to the waist-high music cabinet in our living room to begin bubbling in the answer sheet, the pattern of the sun falling on my idle hands caught my mind more than the questions. The "Age 9–12" version of the test asked about my feelings. Some of the answers were fill-in-the-blanks, and some were multiple choice: "When my (brother/sister) died, I felt: a) angry, b) sad, c) guilty, d) confused, e) lonely, f) all of the above." I tapped my pencil against the side of the cabinet like a rapid metronome. *What did I feel, what did I feel, what did I feel,* I repeated in time to my tapping pencil. *What did it feel like to have a little brother die?*

The day we found out Jacob had cancer was hot, smoggy, and yellow. Mama had left a note telling us that she had taken Jacob to get some hospital tests done, to be good kids, and to do our piano practicing and homework. So of course we were out in the backyard, our school bags thrown on the kitchen table, and our piano books

---

Naomi Frandsen *grew up in La Canada, California, the third of eleven children. Her parents led her by example to a love of reading, learning, and the Church, all of which she still enjoys as an English major at BYU. She hopes to serve a mission in 1999.*

unopened. When the phone rang, Rosalynde ran to get it—she was the oldest. Gabrielle, Brigham, and I waited out underneath the basketball hoop. Everything was quiet until the backdoor squeaked open again and Rosalynde came out wearing an odd expression.

"Mama just told me that the tests show that Jacob has cancer," she said in an expressionless voice. I felt a sharp stab of something—mistrust? disbelief? alarm?—but I didn't know exactly what *cancer* meant, so I looked scrutinizingly at Rosalynde and Gabrielle in order to know how to respond. They didn't give me much help. Rosalynde ran into the house and started pounding Beethoven on the piano; Gabrielle locked herself into her room. Brigham and I just stood outside, underneath the basketball hoop, waiting to know what to do.

I felt that same blankness when Daddy told us that Jacob was going to die. By this time we were familiar with the cancer routine: Mama spending the night at the hospital, Daddy driving us out to see them during the week, Rosalynde bossing us kids around in the meantime. That night seemed no different. We left the dinner dishes stacked on top of the other dishes from the past couple of days, I took a book along with me just in case we were there for a long time, and we piled into our orange VW bus to drive that well-known route to Children's Hospital in Hollywood.

When we arrived in 4-West—the cancer ward—the attending nurse whispered something to the other family in the room, and they all filed silently out, closing the door behind them. We drew up chairs in a circle around Jacob's bed and just looked at him for a minute. He was as pale and thin as the sheet resting lightly on top of him. His favorite teddy bear, Brownie Bear, looked too big for his thin arms. I looked at Mama, Rosalynde, and Gabrielle watching Jacob, and wondered what they were thinking. Then Daddy began talking in his gentle, serious voice. "Kids, tonight Mama and I are going to tell you something wonderful." Here he paused. His voice had broken on the word *wonderful*. As soon as he began speaking I knew what he was going to say. Rosalynde and Gabrielle knew what Daddy was going to say too, and Rosalynde's head sunk down to the side of the hospital bed where her forehead pressed hard against the cold metal rail, but Gabrielle looked stony and stubborn and would not meet anyone's eyes.

"Jacob has been very sick these past two years and the doctors have been doing everything they know to make him better. We have given him blessings and the ward has fasted for Jacob to get better but he just keeps getting sicker and sicker and keeps hurting more and more. Well, Mama and I have talked to the doctors and they told us that they think Jacob will not be here much longer. They've told us that his body is getting tired of fighting against the cancer and is worn out with the treatments. And so, kids, something wonderful is going to happen." Rosalynde was crying. I could see her body shaking against the bracing metal rail. Mama's tears came out as if fighting against her, as if every tear was a razor blade cutting through her cheeks. I still watched, not knowing what to feel.

"Heavenly Father is going to take Jacob back pretty soon and Jacob will no longer be hurting or be in pain. His body will be new and whole and it won't hurt him anymore." Here Daddy stopped. None of us said anything for a long time, so I just watched everyone else, marveling when I noticed Brigham crying too, wondering how exactly they could make themselves do the right thing at the right time. I knew that I should probably be crying too—Anne of Green Gables cried when she thought Gilbert was dying. But inside I just felt empty, blank, dark: nothing.

Because I didn't know how to act or feel about his illness I would sometimes draw Jacob into my own world of pretend and imagination. The first Christmas that Jacob was sick, Mama decided that we should go Christmas shopping as usual; and on our annual trip to the Glendale Galleria I got to be Jacob's partner. After looking in all the pet stores, toy stores, and bookstores, we happened past a McDonalds. Jacob was pretty skinny at this point, and I thought french fries would be a nice treat after those disgusting muscle shakes he had to drink. As we waited in line I held Jacob against my hip and pretended that I was a grown-up and Jacob was my little boy. Looking around at the other people in line, I wondered if they would think I was Jacob's mother. I decided that if they asked me, I would say yes and that my husband was a doctor at Children's Hospital, so I had to do all the Christmas shopping. When my turn came I glanced slyly up at the cashier to see if he was impressed with my grown-up air as I carefully counted out forty cents and laid it on the stainless steel counter top. The cashier seemed oblivious to my sophistication, but as I walked to the booth with Jacob I decided that was because I was so convincing.

When we met Mama thirty minutes later in the International Toy Store I proudly told her that Jacob had eaten a whole packet of french fries. When we got home Jacob felt sick and went to lie down on his couch. While Mama hovered over him, I curled up a distance away in the rocking chair. Mama was the grown-up now. Not five minutes later Jacob cried out in his high, thin voice, "I need my base-man, I need my base-man!" Mama grabbed the nearest basin and ran to him. Bending over, his face contorted in pain, Jacob vomited. The yellow, mushy, partially-digested french fries matched the yellow color of the bottom of the basin. The odor of his vomit nauseated me, and I ran outside to my backyard fort until Mama called me in for dinner.

Although I avoided the reality of Jacob's illness, I couldn't pretend away the complete lifestyle change that went along with it, and I knew very well that I didn't like some of those changes. As Jacob got more sick, Mama would divide her time between home and hospital. We would sometimes see her after school just as she was backing the bus out of the driveway, but for the most part we got used to long notes taped to the front door telling us what was going on that afternoon, what to eat for dinner, what not to do. The notes always ended with "Be good kids. Love Mama." We would take off the note and glumly enter an empty house.

There were other side effects of no mother: Rosalynde was in charge. But because Rosalynde was also going to school, she couldn't do everything that Mama did. Rosalynde couldn't fix my hair every morning, so sometimes for three or four days my hair would stay clinging to the French braid Mama had done for Sunday church, growing more messy every day. But I didn't mind that too much. What I did mind were the lunches Rosalynde packed. They were the same every day: a mushy apple, some broken graham crackers, and worst of all, a peanut butter and granulated honey sandwich. I could eat a couple of bites of the apple and I always liked the graham crackers, but when I unpacked the sandwich, already looking stiff and dark from the honey that gritted between my teeth, I would just throw it away, plastic bag and all, and share my best friend's tuna sandwiches. But sometimes my sack lunch would have a surprise. I would find a note written on the napkin in Mama's minuscule handwriting, and a quarter for an ice-cream sandwich would be taped to the inside of the brown paper bag. And then I would know that Mama had come home after I was in bed and had left before I was up, but had still taken the time to pack our lunches.

I sometimes felt guilty that Jacob was sick, but it's not the kind of guilt you might expect. I didn't have any notion that I had somehow caused his death, and I didn't think that our family was being punished because I had been bad in some way. My guilt occurred on much more local levels. While Jacob was sick we would often get dinners from the Relief Society ladies. Unloading everything from their Suburbans and minivans, their children (my Primary friends) would carry in delicious smelling concoctions of chicken and rice, Jello salads with heavy whipped cream on top, soft white dinner rolls, and best of all, pans of brownies for dessert. I began to look forward to 6:00 P.M. because that's when the Relief Society ladies would start coming. While they served dinner they would talk with Rosalynde as though she were a grown lady like themselves, and discuss with Daddy how Christie is doing in serious, hushed tones. If I eavesdropped on their conversation, I could find out a lot about what was happening. The house always seemed fuller and warmer when they were there, and the unfamiliar casserole dishes and salad bowls lent an exotic feel to washing the dishes. Sometimes, though, I would burst into the house after school and find Mama home. I was glad she was there; things were complete when she was home. But I also felt a little edge of disappointment because I knew it meant we would have to do our piano practicing, and I knew it meant that we wouldn't be getting any dinner from the Relief Society ladies. So I felt guilty. Wasn't it wrong to like Sister Ballard's spaghetti and meatballs, fruit salad, and brownies more than Mama's scrambled eggs?

Toward the end we finally moved Jacob home. In order to take care of him Mama learned to use Jacob's hospital equipment. We installed his "hospital" upstairs in Mama and Daddy's bedroom, and hooking up Jacob's feeding tubes became a nightly ritual in which everyone played a part. Sibling rivalry became the name of the game, because Jacob would want either Rosalynde, Gabrielle, or me to hold him and squeeze his hands as Mama threaded the tube through his nose. If Jacob chose Rosalynde or Gabrielle, I would bring my writing notebook with me and pretend not to notice them for the whole time. But when Jacob chose me . . .

"Naomi! I want Naomi to be here! Where's Naomi?" Jacob's demands were promptly carried out and a glum-looking Gabrielle came downstairs and told me to "For Heaven's sakes get up into Mama's room!" From her cross tone I knew that Jacob wanted me to hold him, and I flounced upstairs feeling very important. As I sat with Jacob on my lap, I looked around at the circle of my family, wondering if they were jealous of me, wondering if they noticed that Jacob loved me more tonight. But none of them were looking at me—not even Gabrielle. They were all looking at Jacob, and at Mama, who was carefully threading the tube down through his right nostril. Jacob squeezed my hands tightly and tensed up his body in my arms.

"It hurts, it hurts, it hurts, it hurts! Stop it Mama, make it stop—it hurts!" Jacob's voice wailed with pain and the tendons in Mama's neck stood out in harsh relief as she concentrated on feeding the line through his nose and into his stomach. My meager hand-squeezes seemed inadequate. What could I do against the vastness of Jacob's pain? After Mama finished hooking Jacob up and we had family prayer, I didn't wait around to taunt Gabrielle. I went quickly downstairs and curled myself tightly underneath my bedspread.

Gradually, Jacob's dying became more real to me. It pierced through the confusion, the avoidance, the guilt, even the rivalry. It pulled me to a place where I could realize his dying without having to pretend it away or sentimentalize it into safety. I found that place one afternoon soon after Mama gave birth to my fourth little brother, Abraham Jacob. When Abraham came home, his bassinet was set up in Mama and Daddy's room. Jacob lay in the big bed, Abraham lay in the ruffled cradle, and Mama sat in the rocking chair between them, watching them both breathe. That afternoon Mama asked me to come up and watch Jacob while she ran errands. I took an apple and a book and climbed slowly up to the big, silent, sick-smelling bedroom to sit in the rocking chair that Mama had vacated. I didn't read the book and I just turned the apple around and around in my hands.

I rocked back and forth slowly, in time with Jacob's breathing. Sometimes I would stop rocking entirely and lean forward anxiously, terrified until Jacob took another slow, thin breath.

What would I do if Jacob stopped breathing? For the first time I thought about that question and looked at my little brother to find an answer. Jacob lay on the bed, his thin arms resting weakly on the pillows that supported him. His dark hair was thick and tousled; it looked too heavy for his head. His cheeks were as white and hollow as if they had been sculpted. He seemed to me like a picture in a glossy-paged children's book, and he had the same pallor as some of the white marble statues we had seen at Forest Lawn when Mama and Daddy were finding his grave site for him. The room that afternoon was dim and yellow and slow. Homework, practicing, everything seemed very far away and unimportant. I went on twisting the apple and rocking the chair, watching Jacob breathe.

On the night of May 2, Brigham and I were camping out on the floor of the living room. When Daddy came to tell us Jacob had died, I followed him obediently upstairs, not feeling or thinking a thing. Rosalynde's red eyes and streaked mascara and Mama's drained grief as she knelt beside Jacob's body seemed like an accusation of my lack of emotion, and I envied baby Benjamin for being able to cry. I didn't stay up very much longer. After Daddy blessed Jacob's body and Mama held us tightly for a moment, Brigham and I walked down to the living room to go back to sleep. When I woke up the next morning I was surprised to find Jacob's dying still true.

I still didn't know what to feel at Jacob's funeral a few days later. We arrived there early, and Mama was carrying a duffle bag with combs, toothbrushes, and books to keep us in order. Rosalynde, Gabrielle, and I sat against the wall of the Relief Society room while a long line of people filed past us to look at Jacob's body lying close by. I accepted hugs from the ladies going past me, I told everyone who asked that I was doing okay, I smiled at the little jokes intended to cheer us up, I got bored of sitting and waiting, I posed for pictures.

One of those pictures haunts me. Some kindly Relief Society lady—probably one who also brought over delicious dinners—lined us up in front of Jacob's coffin and snapped our photograph. With one exception, the family is a collage of red eyes, grief-slumped shoulders, and haggard faces. I am the exception. Dressed in my favorite hand-me-down, rose-colored dress, I am smiling brightly at the camera, my brown hair bouncing around my shoulders from the pink curlers I had put in the night before. My family is grieving, my little brother looks like a cold stranger beneath layers of funny-smelling funeral makeup, and I am smiling cordially at the nice Relief Society lady taking our picture.

After the funeral I felt like Jacob's death should be a huge, momentous, life-changing event. Accordingly, I wrote him a poem. Mama put it in a scrapbook along with poems Rosalynde and Gabrielle wrote, and as I read them all I felt the hidden satisfaction of superiority—my poem rhymed, and besides, it was by far the longest. My fancy handwriting took up a whole side of scrap paper. Along with the poems, I also made solemn vows never to let a day go by without thinking about Jacob. To remind myself, I nailed Jacob's initials, JKF, into a piece of wood, and put the little monument beside the front door of my backyard fort.

Soon enough I forgot that everything was supposed to be huge and momentous. I forgot that I was supposed to be feeling sad all the time, so after only a few more bad poems I started talking about Jacob without pulling a simpering face. My life began winding back up after its abrupt stop on May 2, 1989, and I got excited about graduating from elementary school and starting a baby-sitting business that summer with Gabrielle. Normality resumed when we fell into a steady schedule of school, church, piano lessons, soccer games. Jacob was a part of that schedule too, as we visited his grave every Sunday. While Mama sat beside the gravestone with her knees pulled up to her chin, and Daddy stood behind her, a hand on her head, I went for walks with little Rachel to hunt for clover flowers and to pick up plastic bags littering the bottom of the wall. At the end of what always seemed like a long visit we would sing songs together—"I Am a Child of God" and "How Much Is That Doggy in the Window?"—and then we would climb back up the hill to our orange bus, and I would fall asleep on the way home.

After a short while our Sunday visits became every-other-week visits and then just once-a-month, and instead of spending an hour there we would simply clean off Jacob's grave, sing songs together, say a prayer, and then climb back up the hill to the car. Rachel and I stopped taking long walks around the cemetery, and we never could find our way back to the place where all the clover flowers grew. One Sunday after we returned from the cemetery I pulled out the scrapbook we'd put together after Jacob's funeral, and discovered with a sinking feeling in my stomach that my poem wasn't all that wonderful after all.

One afternoon I found my Jacob memorial covered with fallen apricot leaves. My fort was falling down, and in the square of wood, the nails outlining "JKF" were crusted over with brown rust. I realized that I hadn't thought about Jacob at all that day, or the day before. My vow to never let a day go by without thinking of Jacob was broken, and I had even forgotten that I hadn't remembered. The rusty nail heads and dirty wood accused me of negligence, and I responded with a compliant thrust of guilt. After all, wouldn't it hurt Jacob's feelings that I didn't remember him? But the guilt had no staying power. Walking back toward the house to set the table for dinner, I realized that I felt sadder about not feeling sad than about Jacob dying. But that was okay.

It's been ten years since Jacob died. Visiting his grave has become a joyful event as well as a solemn one because it is one of the first things we do when our family finally gathers together for Christmas and Thanksgiving. When we went to Forest Lawn this past year for our annual Christmas visit, I looked at little Benjamin who was eleven, the age I was when Jacob died, and I wondered how he would have reacted to Jacob's death. Would he have written sentimental poems? Would he have smiled into the camera at Jacob's funeral? I am glad I won't have to find out. Jacob's death marked the transition for me between the end of childhood and the beginning of a time where everything gets harder and more complicated. His suffering now seems more innocent than other trials that could have happened, so when I look back at those two years he was sick I feel a little as though I am seeing the shifting, fleeting remnants of an Eden. The pictures show how young we all were—even Mama and Daddy—and how Jacob's death managed to pull us all into an older world. When I was eleven, my little brother Jacob died of cancer. But now I am twenty, and life is still going on.

Chapter Eight

MAX WILL ALWAYS BE MY BROTHER
by The Omerza Family

Max had his sixteenth birthday just three weeks before he committed suicide. He was a straight-A student, had lots of good friends, attended seminary, and was active in the Church, along with the rest of his family. To all those who knew Max, this act of suicide appeared to be completely and totally out of character. Not one person has come forward to indicate that Max might have had this on his mind. It came as a great shock to his family, his friends, his ward, and the students in his high school. Following are reflections from selected members of Max's family about their feelings and grieving processes.

FATHER'S REFLECTIONS (AGE 55)

We were attending fast and testimony meeting when Max leaned over to me and asked what time Nikki's ward meetings started; she attended the singles ward. I told him that her meetings started in

---

The Omerza Family *resides in Mesa, Arizona. Jay, who served a mission in Brazil, is currently the ward Young Men president. Marlene is in the stake Relief Society presidency. Nikki served a mission in Washington D.C., married Layne Rousseau, and lives in Mesa. Marnee and her husband, Keldon Donaldson, with their sons Cameron and Christopher moved this summer to Payson, Arizona. Jason served a mission in France, married Abby Wilmarth, and lives in Indianapolis. Stefani has one more semester at the University of Arizona. Paul is serving a mission in Florida. Max would have been a senior in high school this year. James is a sophomore, Mandi in her first year in junior high.*

about two hours. A while later I realized Max was no longer sitting on the bench with the family, but I didn't give it much thought. The kids are always getting up to get a drink or to go to the restroom. Later someone told me he saw Max sitting alone on the sofa in the foyer during the meeting and noted that he seemed preoccupied. I didn't see Max when priesthood meeting started, but that's not unusual. Sometimes he sat with his friends, so I didn't always see him. When I got home his car was in the driveway. I had asked our home teacher John to come to the house after church to assist me in giving my wife a blessing; she was going to have surgery on her knee. When John arrived everyone began to gather in the living room. We were all there except Max, so I went to his room to get him. His door was closed, with a note taped to it that read "To whom it may concern." I opened the note and read it.

> I have taken on the ultimate question. Is the Church true or not? I decided to go and find out. This is the only method that will work, in my eyes. I have to know. There is too much pressure in the world today. I don't want to be a part of it. To all those I have caused harm, I'm sorry. I will find the truth soon enough. Farewell to all. Max

I thought the note was a bit strange, but it never entered my mind that it was a suicide note. I figured at first that Max had gone off somewhere to be by himself, but I recalled seeing his car in the driveway. I went outside, and there was the car. Puzzled, I walked back toward Max's room and read the note again. I knocked on his door. There was no answer. As I reached for the doorknob a bad feeling suddenly came over me. I opened the door and found Max lying on the floor. He had shot himself with my rifle. I knelt down beside him and put the back of my hand against his cheek. It was cold. "Oh, Max," I whimpered.

I ran back to the living room and motioned for our home teacher to come with me. I handed him the note and asked him to read it. We entered Max's room. John put his arms around me and began to sob. "Oh Jay, I'm so sorry," he repeated over and over. I just stood there. I couldn't cry. I couldn't speak. I was completely numb. All I could think of was, "I've got to bring him back."

John ran out to get the bishop and the stake president, both of whom lived just a few doors down the street. I stood outside Max's room until the other men arrived. Having surveyed the scene, the bishop said that the police would need to be called. "Before we do that," I said, "I feel an obligation as his father to try to call him back. Will you help me?" The stake president recounted these next moments in his address at the funeral service:

> Jay asked the bishop, his home teacher, and me if we felt we could assist him in an administration to Max. It was the natural, heartfelt desire of a loving father that, if it were at all possible, Max could be restored to life. It was approached with the sweetest acknowledgment and expression that the Lord's will must be done—that whatever the Lord felt was best for Max was the right thing to do. Together we went into that room and knelt around Max. We heard such a sweet and fervent petition and blessing of the priesthood. The blessing was given in the spirit that the Lord's will is what we all most desired. We knelt quietly for a few moments following that blessing, and an overwhelming spirit and a feeling of peace, comfort, and calmness entered as I knelt there beside Max and held his hand. There was the clearest impression to my heart and soul of Father in Heaven's love for this boy. It was almost as though I heard the words, "I love this son." The peace and the comfort that were in that room radiated throughout the home.

This was the first of many spiritual experiences and feelings of great wonderment for me. I was completely devastated, yet each time I entered the room I felt a great feeling of peace. At the time I questioned my feelings. *How can you be so cold and uncaring? Your son is lying here dead. How can you possibly be feeling any peace at all?* Upon further reflection of those moments I have concluded that there must have been people from the spirit world waiting there in the room to comfort me. I have no other explanation.

From the moment I opened the door and discovered my son lying on the floor, I began to feel as though I were taking a bath in Novocain. I was numb, yet fully aware of what was going on. Breaking the news to my immediate family was not easy. How could I break this kind of news gently? Should they go in and look? Should my son come home from his mission? My heart was breaking into a million pieces. How could I help them when I couldn't help myself? I've read a lot of things since then; many of the things I did were done "the wrong way." But if I had it to do over, I don't know if I could do it any differently; it all happened so fast. I do believe we must rely on our feelings and allow ourselves to be guided by the Spirit. We must discuss our feelings openly with each member of the family, but always allow each individual to decide for him or herself. I was very fortunate; I had been fasting that day.

As the word of Max's death spread, many people came to our house—nearly one hundred that evening. They looked at me, I looked at them, but we didn't know what to say to each other. They simply put their arms around me, pulled me in close, and held me long and tight. I knew what they wanted me to know. Then Max's friends began to arrive. I saw a reflection of myself in them. I could see they were aching inside and searching for answers just like me. I felt prompted to go and do for them what was being done for me. But I said to myself, "How can I do this? I don't like to be hugged and I don't like to hug others. Besides, I don't know what to say." Yet I had been greatly comforted by the embraces I had received. I realized I had a choice to make. I could either remain in my shell—in my own numbness—or I could follow this invisible hand that was urging me to give comfort. The choice was mine. To my amazement, as I followed this invisible presence that seemed to be leading me so gently, words of comfort came to me. I felt at peace putting my arms around these kids, many of whom were complete strangers to me. As I gave comfort, I felt a great desire and need to give even more comfort to others. Soon I began to comfort those who came to comfort me.

Another example illustrates the importance of allowing oneself to be guided. The morning after Max died, a neighbor came over and asked if he could replace the carpet in Max's room that afternoon. My initial reaction was, "Do we have to do this now, today? I just can't do this." Then the thought came to me, *So many people want to help. You must let them help.* I reluctantly agreed. I was so glad I had listened. That one act of service paved the way for a tremendous amount of healing to take place with Max's friends who would visit later. It allowed them to come into Max's room and remember him without a morbid reminder of his death.

The following day our family went to LDS Social Services for a counseling session. At one point in the session, the counselor tried to help us understand our feelings. He said that when we love someone, we expose ourselves to be hurt by that person. The more we love, the more we expose ourselves to the potential for pain. Love and the potential for pain are always in balance. He held his hands about a foot apart and said that when somebody we love hurts us, our natural tendency is to close up. He demonstrated by moving his hands close together. We say to ourselves, "Last time, I opened myself up to love, and that made me vulnerable to pain. I'm never going to let that happen again." When we close up, we compress all that pain in a much smaller space, thus it hurts more. The way to reduce the hurt is to spread the pain over a bigger area. But how do we do that? We increase our love. He demonstrated by moving his hands farther apart. We loved Max, and he hurt us. Now we felt pain. We had to choose whether to concentrate the pain by reducing our love or to dilute the pain by expanding our love.

That night the Relief Society had its regular Homemaking meeting scheduled. They changed the format and asked the bishop to come and talk to them and answer questions. When the bishop mentioned this to me I felt prompted to go with him. I was too tired, but I felt strongly that I needed to be there. At the meeting the bishop told the sisters that he had the impression that Max was okay. One of the sisters said, "It almost sounds as if Max took the easy way out. I mean, when you say he's in the arms of the Savior now . . ." "Now wait a minute," the bishop said. "I never said Max was in the arms of the Savior. Max is not in the celestial kingdom. He may still be able to get there, but he has a long way to go. He is certainly not in the arms of the Savior." I felt prompted to say something. I stood up and said:

> I believe that when Max died, he was welcomed into the spirit world by people that love him. I feel like my mother and father, who have already passed on, were there to meet him. I think that pretty soon after Max got there they said to Max, "Now we'd like to show you something. This was the path you were traveling during your mortal

> life. Over there was your destination and over here was where you left the path. You can't travel on that path anymore because you don't have a body. You can still get to the destination, but now you have to follow another path, which is much longer and much harder.

After I sat down I realized that what I had said had come to me as inspiration.

We had planned to have the viewing on the same night as the Mutual activity for the youth. The bishop told me that he was going to meet with the kids at Mutual and have "a rap session." We scheduled the viewing so there would be no conflict with Mutual. Nikki, Jason, Stefani, and I felt that we needed to be at the Mutual activity even though we were very tired. The bishop was talking to the kids when the question was asked, "Is it true that if you commit suicide, you can't get into the celestial kingdom? If it isn't true, then why are we taught that?" The bishop turned to the stake president and asked him to answer the question.

The stake president stood and said, "In some situations, committing suicide will keep a person out of the celestial kingdom, and I think that is why we are sometimes taught that." He then read about suicide directly from the Church's *General Handbook of Instruction*. It essentially says the same thing that Elder M. Russell Ballard wrote in the October 1987 *Ensign*: "Suicide is a sin—a very grievous one, yet the Lord will not judge the person who commits that sin strictly by the act itself. The Lord will look at that person's circumstances and the degree of his accountability at the time of the act."[1] We don't know how the Lord will judge, and it is not our place to try to do so. The stake president explained that the Lord would take into account Max's age, state of mind, and the extent of his testimony when judging Max. On judgment day we will all recognize that the Lord's judgments are fair.

When the stake president finished, he asked us if we wanted to say anything. My daughter Stefani said, "I think sometimes there's a lot of pressure in the Church to find out if the Church is true." She continued:

I think Max was feeling this pressure, and I know what it's like

> because I've felt it too. Our parents and advisors are always telling us to find out if the Church is true because they're worried about us. They want us to know so that we have that knowledge to help ourselves. The thing is, building a testimony of the Church doesn't happen all at once. I think that's what Max thought he could do. He said to himself, 'I want to know right now.' The problem is that getting a testimony is a process. It's not going to happen right now. It takes time.

As Stefani spoke, I listened to her in awe. Her voice didn't crack as she stood there bearing testimony by the power of the Spirit. We were all very tired but we were richly rewarded for making the effort to be with the youth that evening.

Jason and I both felt strongly that we had to speak at the funeral. Neither one of us was sure if we could get through it, but we knew we had to try. One of our main concerns was that Max's friends might take Max's suicide as a signal to do the same. We decided to have the funeral in the afternoon after school was out so that Max's friends could attend. We tried to make sure that the kids would have an opportunity to talk to each other after the service and the next day in school. Jason remembered that talking to his peers had helped him sort out his own feelings after a friend's death.

Many people have asked me how I was able to do what I did that week. As I reflect back upon the events of that hectic period, I realize that it was as if I had been picked up and supported by a large wave in the ocean, carried clear up to the beach, and gently deposited upon the sand. I had been propped up by an invisible hand that supported me, guided me, and gave me utterance. After the funeral was over I was left alone to ponder what had just transpired during that intense week. I began to ask, "Why?"

Why didn't I see this coming? Why didn't Max talk to me? Why didn't I spend more time with him? Why wouldn't the Lord let him come back? Why did Max have to do this to our family? Why won't the Lord send a messenger to let me know how Max is doing? Why can't I cry? Why did Max have to be such a jerk? Why can't I have that feeling of peace anymore? The more I asked "Why?" the more bitter I felt. When I prayed, the words seemed hollow.

I plead with the Lord to help me sort out my feelings and emotions; I didn't like these dark feelings. I began to see that my feelings fell into two groups. One group was sadness, loneliness, grief, and emptiness; the second group was anger, hate, resentment, guilt, and betrayal. The first group will always be with me, but time will soften those feelings. The second group was generated from within me and was closely tied to forgiveness. In order for the second group of emotions to go away, I had to unconditionally forgive Max, ask the Lord to ask Max to forgive me, and ask the Lord to remove these dark feelings from me. I also came to realize that answers to many of my questions had already been given. Answers were given to me each time I attempted to give comfort to others. Now I needed to listen and ponder what I had said to others.

I know that if I had not been willing to follow those promptings to comfort others I would not have had a lot of the answers that I have today. The Lord gave me grace as I gave grace to others. I still miss Max very much, and I cry from time to time. I cried a lot while putting this chapter together. Now I try not to ask, "Why?" I still don't have all the answers that I want, but I have been given all the answers that I need for now. I'm okay with that.

Mother's Reflections (Age 51)

In retrospect I see that the Lord was preparing me during the earlier part of the day for the events that were to follow. The opening prayer in fast and testimony meeting was given by a woman who didn't know me very well, but the prayer seemed very personal. She asked Heavenly Father to bless me specifically and to let me know how many people loved me. The sacrament hymn was "He Died! The Great Redeemer Died," which is about the great Atonement of Jesus Christ. A strong conviction came into my heart and soul that the Lord really loves us, that He paid the price for our sins, and that He took upon Himself our pain and sorrow and the heartache that comes from the choices that others make. I had to send Mandi to get tissues to stem my tears that came fast and hard during the hymn.

When we arrived home from Church, I sat on the couch waiting for my husband and our home teacher John to give me a blessing. When Jay came back into the living room after going to get Max, his face was completely drained. I knew at that moment that Max was dead. I don't know how; I just knew. As John went out the front door to get the bishop I asked, "John, is he dead?" John just said, "I have to get the bishop." The impression came even stronger that he was dead, and I started to cry. Mandi and James sat on either side of me, not sure what to make of the situation.

I had a difficult time deciding whether or not to go in to see Max. I knew I was not prepared to view a scene which would be hard to ever forget. I chose not to see Max at that time, but to remember him the way I had last seen him alive. I have never regretted that decision.

As people arrived at our home I realized that none of the members of my immediate family was in a position to help or comfort me. I needed someone to help me cope. My thoughts immediately turned to my sister-in-law Madge, who has been so close to me all of my married life. I asked Nikki to call her. Madge's first reaction was that of disbelief. How could she help to comfort me? She came nevertheless. I needed to voice some of my feelings to her when she arrived, and she was helpful by just listening. I reminded her of a conversation we had had a few days earlier. I had remarked about how happy I was because all of my children seemed to be on track in their lives. They were all working hard and they were all active in the Church. I had wondered aloud if my "Gethsemane" in life was going to be the arthritis in my knees or if I would have to endure other trials. At that time I couldn't imagine a trial much worse than my arthritis. After I reminded Madge of this earlier conversation I started to sob. I hadn't meant to bring a greater trial on myself. I realize now that it was absurd to think that the Lord would test me by having my son commit suicide. I do believe, however, that the Lord used this experience to help us grow.

Neither Jay nor I slept that first night. When the sun came up in the morning I said, "It's real, isn't it?" and he said, "Yes, it's real." I kept thinking that maybe I could just wake up, and it would be nothing but a bad dream. I could not imagine that Max was gone for good. I kept expecting that he would turn up if I just waited long enough.

During the days that followed I kept expecting—hoping, really—that he would come home from school or that I would go into his room and he would be there. But he didn't, and he wasn't.

When Nikki called to tell my parents, they were stunned. They said they hoped that Heavenly Father could forgive Max. In years past the Church has been ambiguous about the position of a person who commits suicide. My parents shared the view of many that the person who has committed suicide is "damned to hell." I believe in recent years there has been a softening of that attitude, as reflected in Elder M. Russell Ballard's *Ensign* article. The thought had never occurred to me that perhaps Heavenly Father could never forgive Max for what he had done. I think that only Heavenly Father knows what Max was thinking at the time of his death and that it is not our responsibility to judge him in any way. When I spoke to my parents myself, they told me that they had not told anyone about what had happened and that they would keep it to themselves. Once again I was completely at a loss. I told my parents that they could tell anyone about Max's death and how it had happened. We were not ashamed of him—only saddened by what had happened. This continues to be our attitude. It has definitely brought our family closer together.

One of the many friends who came to comfort us shared an experience of a nephew who had also died from suicide. Her nephew's family would not talk to anyone for days after the death. They have had a very difficult time healing from the experience and do not wish to discuss it even now. Our experience has been just the opposite. By helping others come to terms with Max's death we have helped ourselves. Sharing our testimonies of the plan of salvation and the part that it has played in our peace with Max's death has helped us to heal.

Another friend told me that music would help to heal me. Another friend had written the words to a song as a commemoration of *The Family: A Proclamation to the World.* When we thought of music for the funeral, I knew that the song had to be included. Those words have become a part of me since that time. With permission, I quote the words here in hopes that they will bring comfort to someone else as they have done for me:

The Proclamation

Father, when you sent me here and said, "Come follow me,"
You drew the veil, and knew so well the trials life would bring.
But your love could not forsake me through my journey here on earth
So you helped me choose a family that is mine through heavenly birth.

In our premortal existence, we knew and worshipped God.
As spirit children we rejoiced as an heritage to the Lord.
But now mortal life has claimed us, and through divine design
Happiness is found in loving homes like yours and mine.
My family ordained of God is my eternal destiny.
The Prophet has proclaimed these truths for all the world to see.
My family is the center of our Heavenly Father's plan.
A righteous loving family is God's special gift to man.

(Jamie Rohner)

During the viewing I did quite well. It has always been a source of surprise to me that the grieving family comforts the people who come to the funeral instead of the other way around. This was the pattern for us. Jay spoke to the young people, comforted them, and helped them with their feelings. I helped people to see that, in spite of the tragedy that had occurred, our testimonies were still intact, and we were moving forward. All of my family participated in the funeral in one way or another except Mandi and me. Our main job was to cry, and we did that quite well.

In the weeks that have followed Max's death, I have often wondered if there was something I could have said or done that would have changed the course of events. For a while I blamed myself for his death because of some things I had said to him that day. I felt that what I said could have driven him to do what he did. I still feel that perhaps I could have handled my conversation with him better. But the Lord has given me the peace to know that what I said to him I said out of love and because I wanted him to change for the better. I had no idea what events would follow.

Although I do not know for certain where Max is or what he is doing, I have found peace through the words of Virginia Pearce from the April 1994 General Young Women Meeting: "Heavenly Father and Jesus Christ live, and they are in charge of this world. They know me. They love me. They have a plan for my future. I will obey the commandments, work hard, and trust in their plan. Sooner or later, everything will be okay."[2] I really believe this.

NIKKI'S REFLECTIONS (AGE 28)

When I arrived home from church, Dad took me into my room and said, "Max is gone." When I asked what he meant, he said, "Max is dead." I looked at him in disbelief and asked, "How? Where?" "He shot himself in his room," Dad said.

I started crying, and then I got angry. I thought, *What were we doing with a gun in the house? How could we be so careless and stupid not to have it locked up?* Then I realized that this wasn't about a gun. If there hadn't been a gun in the house and Max really wanted to kill himself, he would have found another way. This was about Max, not about guns. Dad tried to put his arms around me, but I pushed him away, saying, "No, I'm okay. I want to see him."

Dad didn't want me to see him, suggesting that I remember Max the way I had last seen him. This time I said, "I *need* to see him," and he relented. As we walked toward Max's door, the bishop also tried to stop me. I just looked at him and thought, *This is my brother and my house, and you will not be the one to tell me what to do*. What I said was, "I need to see him, and I'll be okay." Dad and the bishop followed me into the room. I don't remember exactly what I felt, but I remember thinking Max looked very peaceful. I knelt down beside him, put my hand over his, felt that he was cold, and started sobbing again. "Oh Max, I'm so sorry. I'm so sorry. Oh Max." I turned to Dad and said, "Oh Dad, he won't be with us anymore." Dad held me close for a few moments. Then I placed both my hands on Max's hands and laid my head on his chest, all the while sobbing. Dad pulled me up after a few moments and said that it was time to leave. I wanted to stay and stay. I didn't want to let go of those last few moments with Max. Finally I told Max that I loved him and said good-bye. Seeing the body isn't for everyone, but it was right for me. I was able to start my grieving in private and say good-bye to Max. I needed that time.

The responsibility of calling the aunts and uncles and our grandparents fell to me, so I ended up in a bedroom on the telephone. When I was finished and tried to return to the living room, I discovered tons of people everywhere in the house. It seemed that no matter where I turned there were people wanting to talk to me or hug me. I remember feeling somewhat claustrophobic and thinking, *Don't you people have anything better to do than bother my family at this difficult time?* The more I walked around the house, the more upset I became. I wanted to do my grieving in private, not on display for all these people to see. At one point I thought about asking some of the people to leave. Then I went into the living room and saw people crowded around Mom, hugging her, talking with her, and giving her comfort. At that moment I realized that having all these people in the house was just what Mom needed. Some of my anger and discomfort dissipated. I have since thought that having all those people around might have been good for me too. I'll never be sure about that, but I do know that it felt very uncomfortable at the time.

I hadn't had much of a chance to think with all the people in the house, needing to call all the aunts and uncles, and giving the police the information they needed. The one thing I kept thinking was that Max must have felt so alone and in such great pain to believe that shooting himself was the best option. I hurt inside for Max. Later that evening, after everyone left, the stake president and the bishop talked with us and then offered to give us blessings. As the stake president gave me a blessing, he said, "Max loves you, and he knows that you love him." That was all I needed to hear. Somehow the rest of the details and questions would be worked out; I knew that whatever Max's motivations were, he didn't kill himself because he felt unloved. I have prayed every day since then that Heavenly Father will make sure that Max knows that I love him.

Later that night the bishop and stake president shared with us their impressions that what Max had done would not preclude him from entry into the celestial kingdom. When they said that, I thought they were just saying it to make us feel better. I said to the stake president, "I hope you're right, because I'm having a really hard time believing that right now." I knew the doctrine that had been taught to me all my life—that people who take lives cannot go to the celestial kingdom. I truly thought Max could not be a part of our family in the eternities. I could not reconcile what my priesthood leaders were now telling me with what I believed to be the doctrine of the gospel. This conflict stayed with me for several days.

About a week after Max died I was reading in the Book of Mormon and a passage took on a whole new meaning for me. I had shared Alma 34:8–10 often as a missionary, but I don't remember reading straight through to the next few verses. On this particular day the entire context made so much sense to me. In verses 8–10, Amulek is talking about the importance of an infinite and eternal sacrifice, the Atonement of Christ. Then he goes on to say, "Now there is not any man that can sacrifice his own blood which will atone for the sins of another. Now, if a man murdereth, behold will our law, which is just, take the life of his brother? I say unto you, Nay. But the law requireth the life of him who hath murdered; therefore there can be nothing which is short of an infinite atonement which will suffice for the sins of the world" (Alma 34:11–12).

Suddenly I realized that the Atonement could cover Max's sin. Why would Amulek use the example of murder unless the Atonement was capable of covering the taking of a life? Now, obviously all circumstances are different, and only Heavenly Father and Jesus Christ can decide which sins the Atonement will cover, but that day I realized that I had been limiting the power of the Atonement by assuming that the taking of a life was outside its realm. That passage brought me comfort and peace of mind, because it helped me reconcile the thoughts and feelings my family and I had shared with the doctrine I thought I had been taught all my life.

Marnee's Reflections (Age 27)

I had been experiencing a lot of stress in my life when my dad called to tell me about Max. I had been caring for my ill mother-in-law, having a difficult pregnancy, and feeling torn because I wanted to spend time with my mom after her surgery. My dad's first words were, "You need to sit down." Immediately I knew something was wrong, and I was afraid he was going to tell me that something had happened to my mom. I had been feeling guilty about having to be away from my mom when I thought she needed me. When my dad said Max had shot himself and was dead, my initial emotional reaction was relief. I was so glad that my dad wasn't calling about Mom that I was actually relieved. Thinking back on it, I'm ashamed that I was relieved it was Max who was dead.

I do not fear death. My dad and mom taught me about death when I was young. Using a glove to represent the body and a hand to represent the spirit, they showed how the spirit (hand) enters the body (glove) and gives it life. When the hand is removed from the glove, the glove no longer moves but the spirit lives on and will return to animate the body again. This is death and resurrection. There is nothing to fear.

I have read a few accounts of people's near-death experiences. In my mind I mesh the "facts" of their experiences with my knowledge of the gospel and what happens to our spirits after we die. I have imagined what might happen to me when I pass on to the other side. I like to think that I will meet my grandma, who passed away when I was sixteen. As a teenager I thought she was the only person on earth who loved me unconditionally. I look forward to seeing her again. I believe that Max joined Grandma and also Grandpa, who passed away eight months before Max was born.

I have had several dreams since Max died. In one dream, two days after his death, I pictured Max running through dark woods. He was late for an appointment that he promised he would keep. He was taking an intentional shortcut through the woods because he knew he was late. He did not realize that the woods were not safe. He did not fear the dark because he had a light. As he ran he began to realize that the woods were not safe. Something in the dark was going to harm him. He began to fear. He began to think he wouldn't make it to his destination. Just as his light went out, he saw a clearing. In the clearing the view opened to include a beautiful grassy hill with a mansion. My grandma was sitting on the porch. She looked peaceful, but was anxiously waiting. It was as if she knew he was coming, and when he fell into her arms a wave of relief came over his face. He was safe, and he was home. This dream has comforted me with the thought that Max is safe in the spirit world.

I will miss Max, but I am not despairing. My grieving has not been an outward, obvious sorrow. I grieve over Max's confusion. I grieve because I assume that Max felt frustrated—frustrated that the answers to his questions could not be given during his mortal life. I believe that Max feels loved in the spirit world now, and that comforts me.

Some have reflected that I must be in denial of my brother's death. Some have commented that I must not love my brother, or anyone for that matter, because I do not grieve for my brother—my brother who took his life when he was so young. Some have expressed their dissatisfaction at my lack of tears. I have even heard some say that I must think that suicide is an acceptable form of death.

Is it wrong for me to have faith in the resurrection? Is it wrong for me to have studied scriptures and other books regarding what happens to us after we die? Is it wrong to believe that Heavenly Father loves me and my brother and that He will forgive us because Jesus paid the price for us? Of course not. I have faith. I do not fear.

Jason's Reflections (Age 25)

When I received the phone call from my dad, I lost control. *Why?* I thought. *What could have been wrong with Max? What was he thinking?* Shock and sorrow enveloped me. This wasn't supposed to happen to me again. What had I done wrong? Hadn't I passed on my understanding of the importance of life to my brothers and sisters? Why would Max do such a thing? I began to fill with rage. I thought that I had better pray for Max. I knelt down and closed my eyes, but I couldn't do it. My mind was filled with ideas that the Church had caused Max's death. How could I pray to a God whose Church caused my brother's death? I couldn't do it! The realization of what Max's death meant became more and more clear. I would not see Max anymore during this mortal life. He was dead. I was so angry with the Church for making Max feel suicide was the only answer to his questions.

As my wife and I drove to my parents' house I started to think about the rest of the family. My poor mother—how will she take this? What about Paul? This has got to be one of the worst things that can happen during your mission. I didn't know if I could handle this. As I walked toward the front door, I saw my family's bishop. He walked over to me and put his arms around me. Some of my anger started to melt as he said to me quietly, "I love you, Jason. I love Max. I love your family. I love you."

My mother cried when I saw her. I cried too. She mentioned my friend who had died. She asked me for some words of encouragement. I found very few. I didn't feel as though I had any insight into coping with suicide. My friend's death had been very hard on me, and this experience was even worse. I felt weak, angry, and confused. I was no better prepared for this than I had been before.

When I saw Max's closest friend, Phil, I knew exactly what he was feeling. He sat there with a look of bewilderment, shock, and disbelief. I knew that he, like the rest of us, just wanted to wake up. He wanted to wake up and realize that this was all just a bad dream. So did I. I wanted it all to be a bad dream, but it wasn't. This was real. I realized that I had something to share with Phil. I realized then that I would have to use Max's death as a learning experience for all of Max's friends, just as my friend's death had been for me. Even though I felt, and still feel, inadequate assuming the role of a comforter, I knew that people would look to me for advice. I asked Phil to come outside with me. I briefly explained to Phil what happened to my best friend seven years earlier and how it affected me. I told him that he or Max's other friends could call me if they needed to talk to somebody. The next day I knew I had to talk at the funeral.

That night I asked the bishop to give me a blessing: "Please bless me not to be angry." I still felt angry with the Church for, as I had assumed, making Max feel that there was no other solution to his problems. I felt better after that blessing. I have since realized that nobody could make Max do what he did. He made a conscious decision that is in contradiction with the teachings of the Church. What Max did was his own decision; nobody else was to blame. I often read in the newspaper about the families of people who die in accidents. The families try to blame anybody other than the deceased for the death. I guess they figure that blaming someone else makes them feel better, but I think they usually just end up feeling bitter. I have accepted that what Max did was his own fault; he made a mistake. That doesn't make me love him any less.

James wanted to spend the night at the neighbors, so I walked down there with him. I talked to him on the way. It was very obvious that he was angry. Unlike me, however, James was mad at Max. I reminded James that Max is and always will be our brother. I told him, like I told Phil, that we should learn how important life is from this incident. When I got back to the house, Mandi said to the rest of us, "You know what? I didn't need a blessing because I know that Max is going to be all right." Tears welled up in her eyes and she started crying. She sat between Mom and me, and we hugged her. It hurt me so much to see how much pain James and Mandi were going through. Oh Max, can't you see how much we all love you?

Late that night we knelt in the living room and Dad asked Heavenly Father to help us through the next several days. He asked that Paul and Marnee be blessed as well, since they weren't with us. He then asked Heavenly Father to take care of Max and to let him know that we love him. We all cried.

When Max's friends came over to the house I invited them to come back to Max's room, assuring them that the carpet had been replaced and the room had been cleaned up. They came in, and I told them about how our neighbor had changed the carpet and how we had rearranged the furniture so that it wouldn't be so hard on Mom. I told them that we could remember Max without being ashamed to be his friend. "Max will always be my brother, and I will always love him. Max will always be your friend. Just remember that what he did was wrong. Learn from his mistake." I left the boys to sit in Max's room and think. They were silent as I left.

Max's friends left about an hour later. They were happy; they had been talking about the good times that they had shared with Max. They came back several times; they even brought Mom some roses. I think they understood the message that I wanted to communicate to them. We don't have to be ashamed to have known Max because of the way he died. Max is still our friend, brother, son, cousin, and nephew, no matter how he died. It's okay to talk about him, and it's okay to talk about the way he died. We must learn from him, though. We must learn that life is a precious gift.

At the dedicatory prayer at the graveside I felt the peaceful calm that Dad had talked about so many times. I knew that I would see Max again. Jesus prepared the way for all people to be resurrected, no matter what. After the prayer I walked over to where the casket rested above the grave. I looked at the headstones of my grandma and grandpa next to where Max would be buried. I placed my hand on his casket. Max's body will be safe there until he is resurrected. His body will stay there until that part of Max that was so obviously missing—his spirit—is returned. If that happened before I died, I would be able to greet Max there. I could put my arms around him, and we would talk. If I die before the resurrection, I will look for Max in the spirit world. Maybe I'll be able to help teach him and help him progress. Or maybe he'll have stuff to teach me by then.

I will miss Max. I love him, and that's why I'll miss him. That's why it hurts. I know I'll see him again. Max is my brother, and he always will be. I'm glad I was associated with Max here on the earth. I am proud to be his brother. I will never forget him.

Stefani's Reflections (Age 21)

I had just returned home from a fireside Sunday evening. My sister Marnee had come over to talk with me and comfort me. Two days earlier my boyfriend had decided that we should end our relationship of two-and-a-half years. After we had talked for a while, Marnee called my parents. She asked me to come to talk to my dad on the telephone; she told me that I had better sit down. I started to cry as I put the receiver to my ear. I could tell something was very wrong. The first thing I said was, "Dad, what's wrong? What's happened?"

He said, "Stefani, Max is no longer with us." What he said hadn't completely registered.

"What?" I asked. Then he told me that Max had come home from church and shot himself. I started to cry uncontrollably. My immediate response was, "Dad, I want to come home!"

I couldn't believe it. How could so much heartache come to one person and one family in such a short amount of time? My mom was having problems with her knees, Marnee had gallstones, my dad had just gone through some tests to see if he had cancer, and I was heartbroken. I no longer had my best friend—my boyfriend—and now my brother was dead. He had killed himself. And the one person I wanted to talk to about everything had abandoned me two days earlier.

As I drove to my parents' home that night I felt numb. I guess it was the shock of everything. It was so unexpected. Max had been fine. He was a good kid and I knew he'd been trying to be better. I was confused again as I remembered what I was like at age sixteen. Max had come so much further than I had by then. I had also tried to commit suicide when I was sixteen, but something—a greater power than my own—had stopped me. But Max hadn't shown any signs. I would have seen them. He had not been depressed.

So many questions filled my mind. Had I missed something? Why didn't something stop him like something had stopped me? It just didn't make any sense. I felt like Alma the Younger did when he experienced so much pain that he wished he "could be banished and become extinct both soul and body" (Alma 36:15). I wondered what I had done wrong to deserve so much sorrow in my life. When I finally made it home, there was a group of people on the sidewalk in front of our house. I knew most of them. They were people from my parents' home ward—the ward I grew up in. I didn't want any of them to talk to me or even see me. I hadn't cried much during the drive there but as I walked from the car to the front door I started to sob. It was real. Max was really dead. And I knew inside that door was my hurting family.

The door opened and the first person I saw was Jason. We embraced and cried. As I looked around the room into the eyes of my other family members I could see the confusion. Mandi looked the most confused. She was literally clinging to Nikki on the couch. Neither of my parents were crying, and James looked hurt and maybe angry, I couldn't really tell. Many of us got blessings that night, and both the stake president and the bishop assured our family that they had felt that Max was safe. For all the questions I had had, I'd never questioned whether Max was safe. I guess it had never occurred to me that Max could have possibly understood what he was doing, or he would not have done it. I didn't realize the seriousness of what I had contemplated doing when I was sixteen years old.

I didn't know it was possible for people to cry as much as our family did the next few days. At one point my mother asked me if she thought we would ever stop crying. It didn't feel like it. I felt a great need to be by my mother's side—to comfort her. I couldn't begin to imagine how awful she and my dad must have felt inside. I felt like there was a poison, instead of blood, flowing through my veins.

When I was able to sleep at all I had nightmares, especially after the viewing. Everyone kept saying that the mortuary had done such a good job at fixing him up and that he looked good. But he didn't. He looked terrible, and he was so very dead. He'd shot himself in the head, and I felt like I was in a horror movie. It was creepy. James expressed the same feelings after the viewing, from which he and Mandi had left early. My father gave James a blessing that the fear would leave; this comforted me as well. James and I slept side by side on Nikki's bedroom floor that night, but neither of us really slept. I think most of the night I had my hand on his arm or chest so that he would know that I was there and maybe so I would know that he was there.

Several relatives and members of my parents' ward expressed that they were particularly worried about me. My immediate reaction was to pull even farther away. I didn't want to discuss it, I think, because I didn't know how to feel or how to make progress. I didn't know what to say to these people. I didn't think there was any way they could possibly understand this pain, this poison flowing inside of me. I still don't think people can understand exactly how I feel simply because they are not me. But I know that they may have felt parts of what I've felt. I also realize now that God knows *exactly* how I feel, even when my words cannot express it.

As that week progressed, I felt so totally alone. There was a constant flow of people in and out of my parents' home to comfort our family, but I didn't feel close to any of them. I didn't want to talk about it with anyone, which is contrary to my nature. No one could understand my pain. I felt a great sense of confusion. I was trying to do all I could to live righteously, but the things I loved most were being taken away, suddenly and without any warning or explanation.

I received many priesthood blessings in the months following Max's death. It was my way of looking for answers, I suppose, because I felt as if God had left me alone. When I prayed I didn't feel anything but emptiness. I felt that God was shrugging His shoulders and saying, "I don't know what to tell you. I can't do anything for you right now." But the blessings I received told me that God wasn't being insensitive. He was crying with me as I learned some very personal lessons about man's agency and the great plan of salvation. I still don't have all the answers I would like, but I know that God has never left me alone. Like Nephi I know that "He loveth his children; nevertheless, I do not know the meaning of all things" (1 Nephi 11:17), and that is all right for now.

NOTES

1. M. Russell Ballard, "Suicide: Some Things We Know, and Some We Do Not," *Ensign*, October 1987, p. 8.
2. Virginia H. Pearce, "Faith Is the Answer," *Ensign*, May 1994, p. 92.

Chapter Nine

RECONSTRUCTING MY LIFE
by Norma Joyce Michelsen

The death of my husband was completely unexpected. He died less than a week after our first indication that something was wrong. Before that tragic week our lives had felt so normal, maybe even better than normal. In the summer of 1993, Jerry and I retraced our honeymoon by going back to British Columbia and staying in bed and breakfasts, touring, visiting museums, attending shows, and eating leisurely gourmet meals. The trip brought back wonderful memories of how young we were when we married, I nineteen and he barely twenty-two. At the end of the summer, when our four children and ten grandchildren threw us a surprise anniversary barbecue in the park, I felt our forty years together had covered the emotional range—full of ups and downs, but always exciting. Jerry challenged life, and although I didn't always agree with him, I was never bored.

I returned in the fall to the same school where I had taught first grade in the same classroom for over twenty-five years. The second weekend of the school year, we went on a long walk with our close friends Pat and Rich, women in front talking school and children, men in back talking about whatever men talk about. About halfway through the walk, Jerry complained of shortness of breath and a pain in his arm. We all told him to see a doctor. I wanted to take him right then, but when we got home and he was able to rest all the symptoms

---

Norma Joyce Michelsen *married Jerry Michelsen in 1953. They are the parents of two daughters and two sons, and have eleven grandchildren. After teaching first grade for thirty-one years in the same room in the same school in Camarillo, California, Norma retired this year. A community volunteer, Norma spoke at the 1998 BYU Women's Conference.*

disappeared. Monday the doctor told him he needed a change in his blood pressure medicine, so he got an appointment with a cardiologist.

Tuesday night was an open house at my elementary school. Jerry usually went with me and had been working all spring on a handcrafted wooden lighthouse he was going to show the children at the open house. It was a beauty, with a revolving light on top—he'd won a prize with it at the Ventura County Fair. At the last minute he decided not to go. He said he just didn't feel good. He was too tired. I hated to leave him home, but he insisted I go.

He was sleeping when I left for school the next morning. At 10:00 my principal called me to the office. The parent of a boy in my class had phoned. She was also an emergency room nurse and told me my husband had had a heart attack. The speech teacher drove me to the hospital. When I arrived, Jerry was having an angioplasty; in the coronary care unit he was plugged up to a heart monitor.

When I returned to his room with my daughter Cathy and granddaughter Becky he was finally awake. He told us how much he loved us. We were only allowed to stay a few minutes, and could not see him again for hours. The doctor described the seriousness of the heart attack. The angioplasty had gone well, but the next few days would be crucial, he told us. I called my sons. Scott, in Connecticut, said he'd be there the next day. Steve, in Nevada City, California, said he would be home as soon as he could—he arrived at the hospital Wednesday night. Cathy and her husband, Bruce, and Pam and her husband, Rick, came off and on; so did Becky and Ryan, our oldest grandchildren.

Friday morning, Steve, Scott, and I were at the hospital early, waiting to be allowed to see Jerry. The nurses kept saying that they were still doing tests. I wondered why the tests were taking so long. After about an hour a doctor came in the waiting room and asked us to go out into the hall. The doctor told us that Jerry's heart had ruptured. When Scott asked, "Can you fix it?" the doctor replied that Jerry had died.

My sons and I sobbed together and held each other. When my daughter Pam walked in and saw us she immediately understood. We all held each other and cried. The nurse came and asked where we should send the body. "The body"—it was unbelievable. He was *Jerry*, not "the body." I made a decision on the mortuary, then another decision to donate anything the hospital could use.

When all the family arrived we went in to see Jerry. My beloved husband lay there. He had always been so alive and enthusiastic. Now he was cold and lifeless. We prayed together and said good-bye to him, each in our own way. The bishop, Relief Society president, and many of our friends came almost immediately. But everything was unreal to me, a nightmare. I kept feeling I would wake up soon, but the nightmare went on and on. I went into our closet, picked out his suit for burial, and sat in the middle of all his clothes and wept. I couldn't look at his clothes hanging there; they still smelled of him. My daughter Cathy and sister Mary came and packed up the clothes for me. It was many months before I could go through them, sobbing as I gave them away.

We all planned the funeral. Cathy gave the eulogy, Steve played the piano, Scott spoke, Pam gave a scripture. All eight of our grandsons were pallbearers—we even included two-month-old Daniel as an honorary one. Our home teacher gave a prayer. One dear friend spoke. Another friend sang. Our son Steve arranged for the marker, handcarved with Jerry's lighthouse and his mother's painting of a cypress tree.

For me, the funeral was an out-of-body experience. I saw Jerry lying in his coffin, a slight smile on his face. I watched my children speak and play at the funeral, I comforted my mother-in-law, I greeted people and hugged them. Only once in a while did the grief break through. Then the pain would be so extreme that I felt like I had been ripped in half. Most of the time I felt only numbness.

In 1941 my father was murdered, leaving my mother with five small children to raise. After her death in 1989 we found a series of letters she had written to my father that continued for almost fifty years after his death—the first written two weeks later: "Even now, two weeks later, I can't believe it. I chose your clothes and your casket; planned your funeral; attended it; saw you smiling a little as you lay there; and I still can't believe it! You were so very much alive always. You just can't be gone. My darling, how can I go on without you?"

When I first read the letters I felt Mom's sorrow and remembered my own when my father died. After Jerry died I reread the letters and knew her agony, felt the depth of her loss. My mother's grief was a mirror into my own heart.

The weeks that followed Jerry's death were hard. I kept expecting him to walk into the room. I would listen for his car to drive up. I would wake in the night and reach for him before I realized he wasn't there. I cooked his favorite meals before remembering he couldn't eat them, bought artichokes, which he loved and I detest. I could not go alone to familiar places we'd shared; I even started crying in the vegetable aisle at the supermarket.

How Did I Get Through This Difficult Time?

I prayed and leaned on the Lord.

I prayed often to help me get through the day. I leaned on the Lord. I felt comforted by the Spirit.

I kept a normal routine.

I went back to work two weeks after my husband's death. The normal business of teaching thirty first graders could block out for a few minutes the reality of my loss.

I took charge of my life.

I had depended on my husband to make most of the financial decisions. Many people wanted to help me make decisions about things like the insurance money and the trust fund, but I wanted control over my life. I felt that so much of my life had spiraled out of control with Jerry's death that I needed the reassurance my own decisions brought. We owned a fourplex in the San Fernando Valley which Jerry maintained. I have never been a plumber, an electrician, or any kind of a fixer-upper, though I tried at first. When the earthquake damaged our property, I made the decision to put it in the hands of a property manager.

I avoided hasty decisions.

A widow should wait at least a year before making any major decisions. It's not a good idea to sell your house or to invest money without careful consideration. The only decisions I made during this time were with careful thought. One was to let my granddaughter Becky move in with me while she was going to our local college. The other decision was to get a dog and a cat. Both of these worked out well—Becky and I were good roomies and close friends for two years, and the dog and cat have been loving to come home to.

I found friends willing to listen.

I was lucky in having two friends who listened to me. I drove each day to school with Margaret, who would listen and listen to my concerns. Each night I would walk with Pat and talk and remember.

I recorded my feelings.

I wrote down all my feelings and thoughts in my journal whenever I felt sad or lonely. I also talked into a tape recorder, even to my husband. I talked to Jerry all over the house, in the car, at school, and at his grave. My sons and daughters said I looked pathetic sitting on his grave talking and crying. I didn't care. The release was good for me.

When after death the numbness and disbelief wear off, suffering sets in. This does not happen in the same way with each person. For some the shock of death wears off in a few days, for others a few weeks, for some it can be months. It is often intermittent—I would be in denial one minute and in deep pain the next. Suffering contains many strong emotions: pain, panic, helplessness, loneliness, anger, resentment, worthlessness, depression, self-pity, guilt. Every widow doesn't feel all these emotions, but most widows feel some of them. I was never angry, but many of the widows that I talked to were—angry at their husbands, at the hospital or the doctor, at the driver of the other car, at God.

I did share feelings of guilt. "Why didn't I see the symptoms of heart disease earlier?" "Why didn't I take him to the hospital Sunday night?" "Why did I go to the open house when he wasn't feeling well?" And I felt helpless. I felt lonely. I felt depressed. I felt overwhelmed with responsibility. I couldn't concentrate or focus. For over a year I couldn't read a book or watch television. I would drive somewhere and not remember how I got there or why I was going there. I cried most of the time. Nothing felt right. I had lost my identity. The main thing I felt was incredible pain, like I had been ripped so far apart that part of me was missing.

For me, these feelings lasted for over a year. For widows I have talked with, mourning can last for six months, a year, two years, four years—grief has no timetable. It varies so much from woman to woman that all reactions are normal. It took me three years until I felt anything like normal again, although I still have episodes of intense pain. But I can now remember the fun things about Jerry, and the good memories flood back in. I can have joy with my family without missing him so dreadfully. I have learned to live with the loss of my husband. Several things helped me do that.

Things That Helped Me Through the Suffering

I found solace in the gospel.

I read the scriptures, prayed, and did temple work. I found comfort in the knowledge that ours is only a temporary parting, that we will be together again. My husband had been an inactive member of the Church. He had changed from antagonistic to supportive in the forty years of our marriage, approving the temple marriages of our children and supporting a son's mission. He had just started to go to ward socials with me and had friends in the Church. Two years after his death I took out my endowments and was sealed to my husband "for time and all eternity," Scott standing in for his father. I revel in the knowledge that I will be with Jerry forever.

I enjoyed caring friends.

One of the biggest surprises after my husband's death was the fact that most of my friends left. Grief made them uncomfortable. Some see widows as a threat. Maybe your widowed state reminds friends that they may be alone one day as well. Maybe some friends see "The Merry Widow" who might be after their husband. Some may feel that the widow is not whole anymore without her husband—they don't know how to act around us. Many friends want you to feel better instantly, want you to get on with your life. There were few who wanted to talk about my husband, though sharing memories of all kinds kept Jerry in my heart.

So I appreciated the thoughtful friends and family who were still there when I needed to talk—two wonderful listening friends, two supportive daughters who lived close, two sons who visited, called often, and wrote letters, two loving visiting teachers and other ward friends who helped me, three sisters and a brother who showed their concern and compassion.

I found a bereavement support group.

I felt so empty that I looked for a group that could understand. I found a nondenominational bereavement group which met at a local church, and my daughters and I went with high hopes. But it was not the right group—though the people there were in as much pain as I was, all we did was watch videos and play games. I could not relate to the woman who sobbed and sobbed over the loss of her dog.

Later I found the Hospice bereavement group: women and men who had all lost a mate. We had a counselor who helped us share our feelings. All the members of the group were going through what I was. Some were further along in the group process, which gave me hope. I stayed in this group for over two years, when some of the women formed a separate group to go to plays or movies together. Eight of us went on a cruise to Mexico. We call each other, have parties, go out to dinner, celebrate birthdays. We always have someone to talk to who understands.

I planned ahead for anniversaries, holidays, and weekends.

These are for me the most difficult times. Even when I am doing better, a special day can put me back in depression and tears. I made a list of the holidays that meant the most to me and my husband and found ways to make them easier to get through. Sometimes I surrounded myself with people. Sometimes I took a trip. Sometimes I called a special friend. My widow's support group ate out together on Valentine's Day, and had a party at Christmas.

Anniversaries are really tough. On my wedding anniversary last year I went to visit my son in Connecticut. This year I'll be in Norway visiting my sister and her husband on their mission. Weekends I always fill full of plans—Saturday is my errand day, Sunday my church and visiting day.

I got out of the house.

Last year I started doing volunteer work. Jerry and I used to love to go to plays and symphonies, so now several times a month I usher at a performing arts theater, showing people to their seats or taking tickets. Then I sit down and watch an opera, a symphony, a musical, a play, or a special performer. I am helping my community, and I don't feel awkward going by myself.

This year I will retire from teaching. My plans are to be a docent at a local living history museum, to teach illiterate adults to read, to be a temple worker, and to travel. It's wise to start slowly. Trying to be too busy and too involved with activities can cause you to feel overwhelmed and inadequate. You need time to grieve, time to adjust.

I fought loneliness.

Everyone, grieving or not, needs to strengthen old friendships and make new friends. This year I started making porcelain dolls with my friend, and now share the joy of making something beautiful.

I was good to myself.

Every woman needs to watch her health. It was very easy for me to eat a bowl of cereal over the kitchen sink instead of a balanced meal, easier still to forget about exercise. The dog came in very handy for me. His need for a walk a day made me get the walk I needed.

It helped for me to keep a flattering hairstyle and to experiment with new styles. It helped to go shopping and buy myself something pretty. It helped to have a massage—it really feels good to have someone rub my back again when I miss having Jerry around to scratch my back or massage my feet. It helped to get a manicure, and it's a good feeling to have someone else making my nails look beautiful.

The final stage of grief does not come all at once. I am still sad sometimes. I still miss Jerry. I still look at married couples and want to weep for my loss. I remember the rich married life. But I really have no need to remarry to be complete. I am stronger and more independent than I have ever been. I am not interested in the social activities in our stake for single adults, though I do enjoy the firesides and the conferences. But everyone is different. Some widows want to get back in the social swing, some are interested in remarriage.

I am now past the intense suffering I felt off and on for the first three years after Jerry's death. I still cry sometimes. Sometimes I am depressed. Special days remain hard for me. I remember the good times with longing and pain. But it is time now for acceptance—for letting go of the grief. It is time for reconstructing my life. The decision to retire was a hard one. I will miss the teaching part of my life, miss the children and their wonderful parents, miss my teaching companions. But it feels good to have come to grips with the question: "Who am I?" Now an even scarier question arises: "What next?" I've made some plans to answer that one.

I wish that before I lost my husband I had known what I know now. I could have made my life much easier if I had been more prepared. We had a living trust, but I wish we'd put all our documents in one safe place. I wish I'd known more about our finances. I wish we'd kept maintenance records on the car, kept the warranties on our appliances, known the names of service people I could trust. I was glad that Jerry and I discussed organ donations. I got a letter saying that two people in our area now had sight. Another letter thanked me for the bone and skin donations. But I wish we had decided in advance about caskets, burial plots, funeral arrangements, and headstones.

I'm glad I know better now how to help people who are suffering through grief. We need to listen to each other. I was thankful for the people who didn't ask "How are you?" or say "I understand what you are going through." Helpful people didn't give me advice. Helpful people wrote letters of comfort and support. They talked about memories of my husband, about the funny, sweet, and totally human things he did. They let me cry and didn't try to stop me or make me feel guilty. They stuck with me, kept in touch, invited me over, remembered to include me. They hugged me and touched me—one of the things I missed most about Jerry was the hugs he used to give me.

It's been a hard four years, but I have survived. I look back on the first few weeks and remember the feeling of denial, shock, and disbelief—the numbness of it all. I remember seeing Jackie Kennedy walking behind the coffin and know how she felt.

My mother was widowed when she was thirty-one. I heard my mother weep and I hurt for both of us. And yet she led a full life. She raised us with unconditional love, taught at BYU for thirty years, acted in plays, films, and commercials. She was "Mother of the Year" for Utah in 1976 and runner-up in the nation. She was a widow, and she didn't like it. She never got over the death of her husband. But she learned to live with it. My mother's life is an inspiration to me. I know that a widow can get on with her life, can find happiness and fulfillment.

I was widowed at fifty-nine. I still suffer at times from the pain, the depression, the panic, the loneliness, the self-pity, and the guilt. I am a widow and I don't like it. I'll never get over the death of my husband. But I am learning to live with it. I am reconstructing my life.

THE BURNING WHICH IS DEATH
by Robert J. Walker

The tiny room is dimly lit—probably to encourage relaxation. The place and context do not inspire relaxation. One steel chair and the examination table are all that will fit in the confinement. Normally we would have joked about the situation, but we have stepped down off the edge of normalcy to a lower, darker place. Karen lies on the gurney moaning softly, occasionally with the infernal affliction building inside her. I sit silently stroking her fingers, we two secreted away in this dim closet like children waiting. We wait for some great unknown but clearly sinister thing. Eventually the nurse comes to lead her away. She struggles to her feet and down the corridor, still capable of remaining dignified in such crass indignity.

I wait in the half light with those tight walls crushing tighter, searching for some reserve of strength. I am trying to catch up; she is outpacing me as usual. It has been only three days since we went to our family doctor with the distressing symptoms that sped us to this oncology clinic—the speed because she would have it no other way. She moves through life in general, even into the maw of adversity the same way always—straight on and full bore. I would have set aside this inevitability for weeks, one week given over to denial, at least one more to give the Lord a chance to make it all go away. Never her.

Robert J. Walker *grew up in small-town Utah: Heber and Pleasant Grove. He married Karen Swenson in 1960, and they had three children. Karen died of colon cancer in 1981. An architectural designer, Robert is currently married to Judy Wells, and they live in Pleasant Grove.*

I know now after seventeen years why those few hours in that oncology cubicle are incised in memory as they are. That tightly ominous spot marked the end of life as we had known it. That cell with everything squeezed out of it except required essentials portended the coming structure of our lives. The vividness of the memory might also have something to do with the fact that I prayed harder in that room than I ever had before.

After the original surgery to remove the cancerous portion of Karen's colon, we settle into the routine of chemotherapy. *Routine* is a misnomer, as is *therapy*—only *chemo* definitively represents the truth of the process, a weekly aggressive poisoning by toxic chemicals, a systemic invasion that passes through every organ and deep into elements of every cell. On its destructive course the metal poisons every defensive mechanism that nature has provided to rid the body of the invaders that revulse it. Vomiting and retching and pain and sweat and bleeding are never enough, no matter the volume or the vigor. Only time eventually brings relief, and then it is time to submit again.

We are on the roller coaster ride that all those who suffer serious illness know too well. One week we are in that rarified air at the top of the loop, giddy with good news and full of hope, only to plummet through that stomach churning drop to bottom out as indicators turn sour. But it's less like an amusement park ride than subsistence farming. In those times when there is a famine of hope, we cull the meager harvest as gleaners. We sort out those few palatable kernels of hopeful indication and make them our diet. The ration gets more and more meager, and we grow thin in our hope.

I am pushed beyond the range of normal human activity to a level that requires a frenetic expenditure of energy. There is still that mainstream train, its passengers comfortably ensconced in upholstery, reading the evening news, their tickets paid, their beverage in hand, and their supper waiting. But I have been pushed off the train. I am forced to run alongside, flailing for a handhold to keep me upright and out of the wheels. Had Father Lehi come out of this contemporary era, his vision might have been not of an iron rod immovably anchored in the earth, but rather one welded to an engine, running down a track at increasing speed.

After ten months Karen is allowed a break in the treatments. She has been planning a family vacation to southern California's amusement parks. "Where there is a will there is a way," she grumbles at me hotly, just audible enough for my ears only, throwing luggage and kids into the tiny overstuffed Volkswagen bug for a trip I knew we couldn't make. She is weak, taking upon her the look of a cancer patient; but she is determined that normal things be done. We hope the outing will rejuvenate her, as she had always been the leader of the charge on these excursions.

But my memory is of her struggle to make it be like it was, lagging behind our rush to the next ride, one of the three children always remaining at her side. She would catch up with the rest of us, perspiring and grinning at her own breathlessness, and push us on to the next event. Certainly, at this point, it is inconceivable that we might never be quite this way again. That possibility, if it had been entertained, might have made those moments sweeter and fuller in the living of them.

We return to the clinic for routine examination to outline strategy for the next phase of treatment. The oncologist performs an investigative massage, searching for tumor mass indicative of any spread of the cancer, fingers probing softly, gently, across the jaw line, under the arms and across the abdomen, feeling blindly for a coalescence of evil malignancy beneath the skin. I keep my eyes on his face for any change of expression. He asks the nurse to set up X ray immediately.

How could a tumor the size of a small loaf of bread not only have survived but grown rapidly in an environment of weekly chemotherapy treatment which has pushed every cell in her body to the brink of annihilation? The treatment not only has proved ineffective, it has created wide-ranging problems. Karen's bone marrow now has trouble producing blood cells. Our roller coaster hits a very down place. While Karen has the tumor removed, I'm picking up the small pieces left of my faith for reconstruction.

Doctors, who by their self-assuredness buoyed us through the living hell of it all, now fix their gaze upon the floor as they speak. We are empty. How devastated Karen must feel, having tolerated the most excruciating physical and psychological torture only to reach a hollow conclusion, having struggled to maintain enough motivation to continue to submit only to find she is not to be rescued, but that having paid the full, cruel ransom she is betrayed and on the verge of execution. As it has been and will be throughout the entire two-year ordeal, there is from her not a single word of complaint. We exist in limbo, hoping for her body somehow to restore itself. We expend vast mental energy second-guessing all the medical treatment, all the spiritual direction. Does our refusal to accept Karen's death as a possibility deny us insight we might have known had we been open to it?

"It will make things easier, easier to take care of," the doctor's voice trails off. It isn't difficult to fill in the blank he leaves, his usual blunt style escaping him. The muscles tighten across the edge of Karen's jaw as she absorbs the explanation. "Fine, if it is to be done, it can be reversed. You promise me now you will reverse it." The outspoken oncologist is cowed, the fierceness of her reply pushing aside his disposition for total honesty. "Yes, I will reverse it as soon as your systems are strong enough to function well again." It was a soft lie.

Under better circumstances she would have actually enjoyed the challenge the colostomy presented. Given her existing weakness, it only meant further erosion of dignity and independence, one more thing becoming worse. The colostomy is one of several markers along the way which should have directed us toward earnest discussion of ultimate outcome. But I do not reexamine the position of my own faith as to eventual recovery. If she does, she says nothing.

From the onset of her cancer Karen struggled to maintain a balance between accommodating treatment and maintaining life as though nothing extraordinary were happening. Normalcy was practiced as high art. I know she found comfort amidst pain in the sounds of adolescent courtship games playing through the wall of her sick room, her son attending to the normalcy she so longed for. For me it was fierce frustration not to remind them in high decibel anger of their lack of respect for the suffering. She would never have that. Her children simply being children, finding joy in their living, afforded her a measure of consolation.

Down another level, her focus begins to shift. Externalities fade as she centers more and more, settling toward her core. Conditions shrink her interests into ever-tightening confines, as brighter stars collapse back in upon themselves, condensed into profound singularity. She seems to be dissolving the bonds between us, a deliberate act of pushing me and the children away. Part of the isolation I feel is her inability to communicate past the drugs and the weakness. But mostly she requires total capacity of reserve to simply survive. She is imprisoned in her world of pain and struggle, a world we cannot really share. We cannot know her pain. We cannot get inside the grief of all dreams dissolving. We cannot know the distress of total physical collapse. What had been united effort in shared strength crumbles into lonely private battles.

I am left wondering why we have to learn so much about pain, when it is only temporary, only temporal. We did not know pain before we came here and will put pain behind us when we leave, yet we are made to know it in all its imposing generalities and its frustrating specifics while we are here. Other than love perhaps, we know no other emotion so well, feeling it physically at all its levels, discovering it emotionally in all its shades. We know it in ourselves and suffer it in those we love. Why this depth of experience with an aspect of mortality which we fervently believe we shall never be required to suffer again?

Perhaps it is the experience itself. Perhaps as in most of life it is never so much the information learned as what happens to us in the process of learning. Each day life makes of us something a little different than we were the day before. Death of loved ones ups the ante, multiplies the magnitude. One of the ingenious blessings of this mortal contrivance of Father's is that the change can be almost automatic. It doesn't take a great deal of conscious effort on our part, pretty much just large portions of enduring to the end. Through that endurance, with as much grace as possible and some love given and some service rendered, we are made different and we are also made better.

She lies asleep on the couch in the family room, having tired of bedroom confinement. The blankets are pulled up under her chin; she is cold despite September afternoon sun spilling warmly through the window. Her eyes are closed within dark hollows, her cheeks gaunt, the skin at her temples tight and transparent. Her face framed by the soft rounding of the pillow is that of a fragile, frail old lady.

She has lost forty pounds and aged forty years. The roller coaster ride has flattened out to an inexorable downhill coast.

She has refused any further treatment and is now on an "as required" pain medication regimen. The appetite which has been minimal for several months is fading. We have reached terminality. I seem to be able to do little now but participate in her death. For the first time since her original diagnosis, I must set that faith aside which has been cultivated for two years. I must turn from caregiver looking toward ultimate recovery to caregiver looking toward inevitable death.

Somewhere in this terrible shift in the gravity of my life, I must find the strength to discuss this all with the children. I think I am dishonest in that I allowed some hope to creep into the portrayal of their mother's condition, still looking for the miracle that faith, though faint, allows. For that I am a coward. The youngest, my fourteen-year-old, believes what she wishes anyway, despite the truth I try to give her and that she can plainly see.

I am charged by bitter circumstance to make difficult choices. Should I allow Karen to die at home and maintain a more intimate contact? Or should she be moved to the hospital where she might be made more comfortable? She should have a voice in the decision. I sit on the side of the bed running my fingertips across her forehead and along her temple, whispering softly, trying to coax response. Her eyelids finally flutter open and those once-bright eyes smile out, but speech will not come. I have waited too long.

We have wasted too many days expecting that ultimate recovery our faith had assured us of. I was not alone in that assurance; it was primarily hers. The possibility of her never becoming well again, the prospect of death, had never been brought into the light of open discussion. It must have been for her, as it was for me, locked away in a far corner of some darker closet of the mind. She passionately embraced the role of warrior, and warriors speak not of death, lest the act of acknowledgement become the cause. Now the warrior is wounded, and the wound proves mortal. I have waited too long.

We allowed that positive outlook the professionals preached to us to disguise too much reality. The faith she had maintained that a loving Father would not remove her from her family had never been reexamined. We allowed compliance to nurture denial. So the precious hours slipped away. Because it might somehow have supported defeatism or crippled faith, we lost the chance to say what needed to be spoken. Our blind conviction in restoration has robbed us of expressions and interactions which should have been.

Ultimately I make the choice of *where* selfishly. She will die at home. I admit to myself that I do it for me and the family more than for her, and will myself into believing that she would concur or is beyond caring. Cold and dark, typical winter early morning, I lie on the floor at her side of the bed as I have for several nights to better hear her breathing, but a soft whisper now, barely audible. My thoughts run to all those years, all those nights lying beside her, content and secure in the rhythm of that sound, the continuity of that radiant life force. It all draws quickly to a close.

I can tell by the sound and by an intuition I can't explain, almost as though I had been there, done that. That terrible sick feeling wells up inside me as the fact of the matter is made clear, either by primitive intuition or spiritual guide. I had decided some time prior to include as much of the family in the final resolution of her life as we can squeeze into our small bedroom. That decision was based on her feelings for family and I felt I had her approval, even her direction. I hurriedly begin the phone calls, the first to our eldest daughter at school thirty minutes away.

I begin to wonder if I have responded too late as her breathing becomes ever shallower, but the guidance is sure and the family comes in time. Karen died about the time the sun came up.

Even as I put words to paper now, seventeen years later, the crushing singularity of that one moment in time impacts the present like the hurling down of mountains. She opened her eyes for the first time in five days to give me the clearly annoyed look of one removed from higher, more sacred involvements. I had caused her to cough as I tried to moisten her mouth and she died.

Taking all that life was to me and leaving, on wings of light midst—those billowing clouds of glory—she slipped away; picked up her skirts and ran barefoot through my summer meadow in that better place, a place I cannot follow. I am here midwinter alone.

And the two shall become as one. By adherence to commandment or by natural consequence we had, through five years of fiery adolescent courtship and twenty-one years of simmering marriage, become two individuals conjoined, a joining not so much of careful construction, but more as forms of metal molten out of the furnace of our trials.

Now death steps in to tear the pair in half, rips from me the better portion and leaves a gaping wound down the half of me, fringed of split sinew and rent flesh, pumping out with each heartbeat all the dreams of all the tomorrows that will not be. That wound as I imagined it was so physically real I wondered that others could not see it and be aghast. No one ever explained to me that the tighter you grow the bond, the greater the pain at disunion. The more love you discover in the relationship the deeper the wound upon parting. If they had told me, I still would have it no other way.

I call Brook, our youngest, into the privacy of the bedroom to help me wash her mother one last time. I am impressed that she needs one last contact, one last time to help. We speak of her mother's suffering, now complete, and feel that this final bath is under her direction. We wrap her in the bed sheet. I carry her down the stairs and out of her house.

I sit now on that couch where she lay on a warm September afternoon seventeen years ago. Like it was yesterday. No, like it was all my yesterdays. That second Friday in December was unexpectedly mild. Opening the door on the bright afternoon had something of release or emergence in it. I meet Mom and Dad at the cemetery and we walk together among the old family plots. Those which Father controls and is willing to share he carefully points out. He is of a more judicious generation, aware of a sometimes perilous future and the need to prepare for it. These two are older and wiser through our births and the raising of us, our marriages and our own families founded, now having seen past hope and faith to the temporality of graves and stones, a place to lay a body down, a grave to tend. A place for her, a place for me beside it.

We two, who love's full measure
Had just begun to know,
And I too soon am come to tend a grave
And placing roses upon the snow.

Embalmers bring former beauty back to that ravaged countenance, that we might forget what life last endowed her—perhaps better to remember the worst life deals us. Her hairdresser does his tender work one last time. Her sisters each lift and move the locks slightly, more of love than concern for appearance. We stay longer than is necessary, unwilling to leave even this vestige, knowing soon enough even this will be taken away, put away, so damnably far away.

Viewings are an exercise in futility. We gather in lines and speak of what was. Mourning fails as a congregational exercise. Deep loss evokes excruciating pain and love's grief, like all pain, is uniquely and unshareably personal. It is a song we sing solo, accompanied only by individual memories. But we go to the viewing. We put upon ourselves our dark clothes and our dark moods and are carried by powers beyond our own, feathers in the wind.

Those who are grieving have entered the protection of the Lord, the refuge that allows us to go into a kind of spiritual shock, a numbing firmness in which He imparts of His own strength into our sinew, His own power into our resolve. The bereaved are in a place apart, and more often than not are able from that haven to dispense more comfort than they receive.

In all that we are ever moved to do for each other it is the singular, simple person-to-person actions that bear most meaning. The afternoon prior to the viewing, two of the sisters in the ward came to the door with a roast still warm from the oven. That meat sustained us for days when we were too busy or too bereaved to prepare meals. Such acts reflect a spiritual glow. How they survive who do not share the eternal perspective of the gospel I shall never know. I do know that the sweet spirit that sweeps in upon us in that worst of times to embrace and support and buffer the agony is there for us all.

Of all the forces which act upon us in a lifetime, few are more powerful than the death of a loved one in its capacity to change us. As faith is defined by doubt, life is defined by death. It is almost impossible to understand the mechanics of the process; it is nearly impossible reasonably to analyze what we are so intimately enmeshed in. You can't know it until it happens to you, and once it happens to you, you are too close to view with required perspective. But given time, some perspective does come.

With death that comes too early, part of the pain is the annihilation of dreams, crushed hope for a future that now will never be. That would help explain why we grieve so for those little ones who leave us before we can know them, never becoming an individual we have sacrificed for and loved in a bond forged over time, but nonetheless grieved for as the bearer of our dreams. It also explains why twenty years after the death of your spouse, you find yourself while holding a beloved grandchild overwhelmed by a surge of grief as you wonder what her responses, what her thoughts would be were she present, to know the experience of it with you.

After the searing pain of parting has moderated over time, there is another pain one becomes aware of. It is a steady ache that fluctuates to some degree but is always there, a pain that never goes away. I think I find its origin partly in the spiritual nature of things. I have always felt that those loved ones whose presence is now on the other side of the veil nonetheless remain very close to us, in caring and supportive, even directive and protective roles. Though we cannot detect them by any physical means, our spirit knows their nearness. To know that nearness yet be withheld from responding is the source of pain that lasts a lifetime, but only that, thanks be to heaven.

My analysis of the death of my wife would be incomplete without the voices of our children. I was caught up in the work of caregiver and breadwinner and housekeeper (as much as was kept). The children in large part were left to struggle with the situation and their associated feelings pretty much on their own. This is not as it should have been or as I would have had it be, but was a consequence of the situation and my weaknesses.

Brook, the youngest of our children, was bonded in those special ways that last born are to their mothers. She was caught by circumstance at the tenderest of ages to face this traumatic challenge. She was mature enough to see her mother as good and capable in a worldly context, knowing the mother who takes pies to the widows in the ward and who chaperones the high school a cappella choir to New York. Her mother's death is a disaster from which she is still trying to recover, a terrible mistake by God, beyond correction and without explanation. We have searched through the old explanations and devised some new of our own, but she remains largely unsatisfied. I failed to prepare her.

Kurt, our son, was eighteen when his mother died. His mother had a strong connection to her only son and took pride in the man he was becoming. Like his mother he is full of fun and is very much people connected. He busied himself at all the varied teenage occupations, I wonder if to fulfill his mother's wish for normalcy. His thoughts and feelings were kept private, outward exuberance masking the deeper turmoil. This is a characteristic permanently inculcated in his personality. I failed to know his state of mind.

Kriste, our firstborn, was twenty when her mother died. She was living away from home and attending nursing school at the time. Her field of study gave her clearer insight and added dimension to the reality of her mother's suffering with the progression of the disease. Being away from home she was not engaged directly in the futility of the daily battle. I found out later that she needed it that way. She could not bear her mother's agony under conditions she could do nothing to alleviate. She became a professional caregiver partly to assuage the guilt she had burdened herself with. I failed to reach out to her.

The children deserved more of me and better of me. I excuse myself in some degree in that I was ignorant of their needs at the time. The Church didn't do much better. Ours is an organization which promotes the family as its core and sees in the family not just temporal but eternal values. It sees itself as the defender of the family. It needs to act on that vision in more profound ways. Our home teachers during that period are among the best people I know and were sensitive and supportive and consistent in their considerable efforts. Our bishop at the time was as good a man and bishop as I have been associated with. The people in the organization tried their best but simply didn't know quite what to do, how best to serve, just as we didn't know. We needed someone to say, "I will prepare your spouse's supper. You take the next thirty minutes and gather your children and speak to their concerns." Some guidance is required to make certain the suffering isn't wasted but teaches us. I can think of no greater service to families than to support and help direct the learning and power for positive change that is inherent in family member death.

I find in retrospect that I made a number of mistakes throughout the ordeal. The real value of this documentation is sharing with the reader my view of that culpability.

Temper faith with wisdom. I had always tried to teach my Sunday School class of fifteen-year-olds that you don't plant radish seeds and expect fervent prayer to bring forth the miracle of a bed of lilies. In this time of tribulation I forgot my own lesson. You can debate with God over eventual outcome, but faith placed outside His direction is faith wasted. Faith is power, but misdirected faith is power gone astray and incurs wasted time and energy. It pays at the beginning to allow for Father to direct the passion of our faith.

Wisdom would dictate that we apply faith not only to the answering of our prayers but also to the issue of what Father feels that answer might best be. For me, as I am sure it is for others, that best answer comes in veiled and often such vague terms as to make one wonder if it is to be perceived at all. It is often difficult to interpret, let alone act upon with any specificity. Commonly the difficulty is greatly increased because we must act quickly in unfamiliar conditions. Am I really to expect an answer from God or have I been left to my own resources? Probably a fair mix of each, as He sees need to fit the circumstance. So we drift in the current of events, paddling furiously at times under divine direction and just as furiously at other times with no direction at all. There are times when we can do only what we must to keep the little group together and help keep each other's heads above water.

Live life fully, even in the bad times. The worst of our times will be looked back upon from higher perspectives as the best of times, particularly if fully engaged in. Bad times require of us the same zest for living as do the joyful intermissions. Difficulties change us, and the greater our engagement in the process the more profound the change. Paddle like crazy when the occasion calls for it, even if you have no idea as to destination. It just may be that the exercise is an end in itself. Take a little pleasure in drifting, as you probably won't see the scenery or enjoy the context again. The intensity of engagement makes of you something different, and someday something better.

Don't berate yourself. I have spent too much time in the enterprise of self-chastisement. I castigate myself for not being more spiritually sensitive or intellectually strong to know the mind of God and thereby mitigate the circumstances. I should at least have had the sense and sensitivity to put the entire situation in His hands and remain fully optimistic in the outcome while prudently preparing for the worst.

Stay as positive as possible. I have always admired those who could achieve and maintain grace under the most dire and trying challenges, as Karen did. That is an accomplishment I struggle to attain in even the smallest crises. I have little doubt that it is a significant lesson that mortality is designed to teach. For some of us it just seems more comfortable to wallow in the mire and find there the lubrication for that dry, grinding axle. We are those who find life, particularly in its more trying venues, capable of being dealt with only on its darker, more cynical edge.

Feel what you feel. I think that anger at God is healthy evidence of the strongest of faiths, evidence of real concern. One does not waste anger on what he does not believe. I was angry with God. I was angry with the system, but it is, after all, His system. I was angry that Karen's suffering and her courage in suffering had not preserved her. I was angry that her faith and mine and the children's faith and the faith of many others had not kept her here. I was angry that she was gone and that I remained. After several weeks and the completion of the business of tying loose ends, I was very angry that I was not allowed to follow her.

Pray. There are those cathartic measures one must find, if not to heal at least to purge. Some actions need to be taken just to keep the feet shuffling along the path. Prayer is cathartic and comes out of me as variably as the forms heaven's moisture finds to fall. What form will the answer take as it is returned to me? The gentler, nourishing summer rain, soft and misty, or the violent howling tempest bent on testing character and courage?

Let others share the death. I invited family participation at Karen's death partly in recompense for turning away many of their offers to help during the course of her illness. Why I felt their participation diminished my connection with Karen I am not certain. I think that was the reason for not allowing their help. Possibly it arose out of guilt for all I felt I owed her and was struggling to repay—I could not square the record if I allowed outside help to discount my own effort. I have always felt that our progress in any aspect of mortality depends upon the degree of our involvement and depth of our immersion. Finally I allowed others to progress. Karen's mother and sisters bathed and fed her on occasion. I should have allowed it to happen more often. It would have been to everyone's benefit. I simply could not bring myself to share her beyond minimum levels; out of selfishness I denied others opportunity.

I should have reached out for support from those who have been through the trial. Help from those who give of themselves, through organizations such as Hospice, would have been beneficial. I didn't need help with the work, but help from being consumed in the work—I could have used someone who had been down this road to read me the signposts, to warn me of significant turns and the need to discuss the progression of events with the children and with Karen. I wish someone more detached could have injected my faith with some timely reality.

Talk. I suppose even if Karen and I had carefully made a dutiful effort to talk of all those things which needed to be said as our life together was ending, it still would not have been enough to allay all the guilt. There may never be sufficient coverage and connection through discourse, particularly in times of stress, to mediate the guilt. I spend many nights with the ghosts of all those times which might have been. I think the remorse may have remained with me still, even had we said all that needed said, but perhaps now I could find some solace in having made the effort. I simply always felt there was time to do it. But she and the time slipped away.

The burning which is the death of those we love extracts from us what would rise as dross by no other means. The choice of whether that fire is consuming or refining is always ours. "I know that my Father in Heaven will not take me until I have held my grandchildren." That oft-spoken declaration grounded our faith back then. I have now little doubt that she has held each of our grandchildren and does so still.

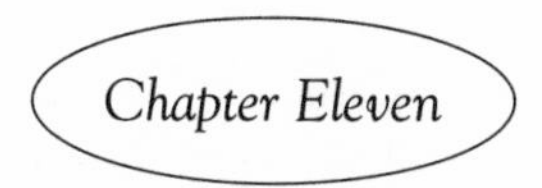

LIVING THROUGH DEATH
by Steve Walker

THE BEST OF DEATHS ISN'T EASY

I'm fifty-six, getting uncomfortably close to death myself. I'm well past the age when we can statistically expect the death of someone close to us, and those same inescapable statistics make the likeliest candidate for death a parent. So it wasn't really a surprise when Dad, three decades older even than I, died last July. Dad "hadn't been at his best," as he'd say it, for years. The time after he began to fail felt like a bonus on his life, a bonus we were able to enjoy for five years. And my father died a good death; his dying went about as well as death can go. He'd lived a full life. He'd lived a good life. He died surrounded by those he loved. He stayed himself until the end, maintained his wit and his courage and his genial disposition.

Jess Walker didn't miss many sunsets, didn't miss many pheasants crowing, didn't miss out on many heaping plates of fried potatoes or boiled cabbage, didn't miss many chances to hug people, passed up few opportunities to sit down and talk things over. One of my friends said exactly what I was feeling at the viewing: "You can't do much more with a life than that man managed." Because Dad himself had

---

Steve Walker *is professor of English at BYU. He lives in Provo with his wife, Ardith, happy to be near their three children and four lively granddaughters. He hopes this book, his fifth, will honor his parents, Jess and Elaine Walker, both of whom died this year.*

missed so little, it came as a considerable shock to me to miss him so much. I'd had so satisfying a helping of Jess Walker that it felt greedy to be wanting more.

Five years ago we thought we'd lost my father; he struggled for his life through an entire weekend, vomiting blood, losing more than I thought any of us had in us, throwing up so much blood we thought we saw his veins collapse. He's small, only 5'4", and looked so frail and vulnerable in his hospital gown that we were sure he was done. His living through that bloodbath seemed sheer miracle to me, marrow-deep grace, and it made me all the more aware that however short the man may be, his soul is stately as Timpanogos, wide as the sky. I felt as if I'd watched him die, then he got to stay longer.

An acquaintance of mine craves just five more minutes with the mother he lost a few years back; I had five final months after five final years to get to see my father almost every day. It seemed increasingly likely that these would be my father's ending days, and that gradual worsening provided opportunity to get up close and personal. Dad was a toucher; you couldn't be around him without his hand reaching out to squeeze your shoulder or pat your knee or hold your hand. Those last few weeks I got to touch him back a little; rubbing his feet in the hospital I got as close as I have been with my father since infancy. I probably hugged him as much in those hospital days as I'd been able to hug him over the past ten years.

Dad died nobly. He was a fighter, my father, and fought the good final fight, even when he got to where he didn't have much fight left. His health had deteriorated irrevocably over the past few years, and he was in a lot of pain from his back broken falling in the yard, out among his beloved roses. The metal "halo" supporting his broken neck bolted into his skull in four places was a source of persistent minor agony, though there was something about that cast iron halo that seemed just right, his kind of real and earthy halo. The pain got fiercer when he slipped and fell in the rest home and cracked his back in another place, lower this time, so it hurt all the way down. He bore even that magnificently, managed the hospitalization and institutionalization with dignity, his good grin intact, his generosity of spirit unsoured.

Not until the day before he died did he become incoherent, insisting in his staunch voice: "You can't do this to me." By that time

I wondered whether his admonition was incoherence or medication, because what we were doing to him by then was a pain reliever so strong it had to be disorienting. They'd tied down his arms to keep him from pulling out the tubes. I'd wanted to pull those tubes out a time or two myself, and I didn't have to endure them as unremittingly as he did, hour after hour. I wondered at that point—as poignantly as he did—how we could do it to him.

He was worn down by the pain. If I'd been the coroner, I'd have listed as the cause of death: too much agony. A few weeks before his death he complained to my brother about the difficulty he was having with his daily therapy. When Robert came in the next morning, he found Dad struggling on the parallel bars to walk, his legs buckled, his face ashen, lips set in a grimace of a smile, the two forehead scars from his halo brace livid with his effort, crimson as drops of blood from that crown of metal thorns he'd endured for two months. The therapist was pleading with him to take a step, just a single step: it was clear that not taking that step meant there would be no more stepping. There was Jess at his best in that ultimate struggle, working to stagger forward, doing his darndest to keep on going when his legs would not allow so much as one more step. My brother Rob wondered how many hard mornings leading up to that day Dad got up and made that impossible step. He wouldn't quit even when it was clear his body had. Robert stopped the therapy.

A couple of weeks later, with family all gathered in his room, we gave him a final blessing. I'm dead set against consigning people to die—think it's a kind of spiritual Dr. Kevorkianism, a refusal to have faith in the face of the final crisis. But all I could think of while I was anointing that wispy white hair was *he's in God's hands*. And when Robert commanded that our father be relieved of his pain I knew, as everyone in that room knew, he was either going to dance off that bed or die very soon. He left us the following Sunday morning, gone when my brother Lynn arrived, obvious peace on his face, Sunday's child to the end, always full of grace.

Much as I didn't want him to die, Jess Walker died about as well as it's possible to die. Even his fierce physical pain, awful as it had to be for my father, was for me a kind of anodyne; the first thing I felt at his dying was relief that his pain was over. My sister Marda dreamed of him the week after his death, striding along, a younger man, legs no longer painful, back no longer broken.

Dad died as he lived, as he did everything: well. And I thought I was ready to have him do it. Yet I was and I am blindsided by grief. Despite all my ease of mind and ease of spirit it is much harder to have him gone than I would have imagined. Sometimes his absence is so crushing I can hardly get my breath. The loss of my father is to me like a profound natural disaster—my brother-in-law Cloyd describes it "as if the wind everywhere stopped blowing." I can't stop wanting to feel his hand on my knee, can't stop needing to talk to him again. I had no idea how much I do in my life I do so I can tell my father. A year later I'm still having to goad myself out of bed some mornings to face a world without him in it. That's too dramatic—it feels less interesting than that. Life is just so much less interesting without my father in it.

My faith makes me absolutely certain I will see my father again, yet it did not prepare me at all to miss him so much in the meanwhile. Driving down Provo Canyon that summer Sunday morning toward where my father no longer was, unable to cry because this grief went beyond what tears could reach, I knew, knew the way you know you are in love or that God is near you, that I will never stop hurting from the loss of my father, ever, until I get to be with him again, get once more to see him smile that crook-nosed grin wide as the sky and put his hand on my shoulder and say just one more time, "How's all with your world, Sonny Boy?"

Not too good, Dad. Not too good with you gone. I'm coming to expect to miss you every day, tomorrow and tomorrow and tomorrow. The overwhelming quality of the grief—the quietly cosmic encompassingness of it, the way it changes utterly the landscape of my most usual living—came as a terrific shock to me.

It is not that I didn't understand a lot about death before Dad died. I knew how death functions for us. I understood death biologically, understood how in a world of reproduction death keeps things from getting too crowded, makes room for new life. If we're going to keep on having babies, somebody's got to go, and the logical choice is old folks. I understood death physiologically, understood that death keeps us from getting too old. If we're going to age, death sooner or later becomes welcome as a way out of our worn bodies. I'm getting old enough that I wake up some mornings lately and think without much sarcasm that I'd feel better dead.

I understood death theologically, realized that death is a transition, a way to get us from here to there, a kind of reverse birth. I always knew death to be necessary in the cosmic scheme of things, even thrilling in the eternal possibilities it opens up for us. What I didn't understand about death until my father died is the personal dimension of death: I didn't understand how much it hurts. The theory's easy—I'm absolutely convinced my father is in a better place, with larger opportunities, happier options, sweeter experiences. But the actual experience is hard. However well I know things to be going for my father, I just don't want him gone:

> One by one the petals drop.
> There's nothing that can make them stop.
> You cannot beg a rose to stay.
> Why does it have to be that way?
>
> The butterflies I used to chase
> Have gone off to some other place.
> I don't know where. I only know
> I wish they didn't have to go.
>
> And all the shiny afternoons
> So full of birds and big balloons
> And ice cream melting in the sun
> Are done. I do not want them done.[1]

It Takes More Than Miracles to Take the Hurt Away

I don't mean to whine. I'm grateful, grateful as an accident victim for morphine, for the comforts that come along with the anguishes. Those comforts are real. I've felt, for one thing, an even deeper appreciation for Dad since he's gone, an even deeper awareness of who he is. I'm surprised to discover that it's impossible to know a person completely until they're no longer with you; I was unable to focus on him clearly because he was too close. It's been gratifying to discover how widely my father was respected. I'm pleased people remember him in ways Dad would have loved and that I do love, such as when a group of my friends, Dad's students at Pleasant Grove High School, instead of flowers gave me exactly what would have tickled him, a case of "Jess Walker Memorial Tennis Balls."

There has been for me, too, in paradoxical complement to that increased objectivity, a deeper sense of Dad's personal presence since he died. My father was fond of saying that he felt closer to his father in death than in life. I didn't like his saying that, seemed to me a pretty poor relationship that got improved by one party to it being dead. But now I find myself, too, closer in some ways to my father in death than before. Maybe it's just because I can't stand the thought of a world without Jess Walker in it, but I think he's still very much with us, very much alive—more than just metaphorically, though I will never see a Tropicana rose nor the afterglow of a sunset nor a red-headed finch, never hear a poem, maybe never think a really good thought without thinking of him. My sister Marda says she can't be sure which thoughts are hers and which are Dad's.

My father was a canny financial planner and instilled a strong saving urge in me. So I couldn't help thinking of him when, the day after his funeral, there came a check in the mail for several hundred dollars, money I needed badly, from a strange, once-in-a-lifetime source: as nearly as I can figure it, an investment company closed out and settled with BYU for more money than individuals had vested. Seemed odd to me. It looked like to me Dad was up there cooking the books to get me some bucks.

I passed that off as coincidence. But the next day, on a crucial writing task, I suffered serious writing block and could not for hours figure out even how to begin what I needed to say. Missing Dad, I went for a walk to the edge of campus to indulge my sadness at his passing. Whereupon there came to me, flooded in upon my mind, ideas for the project—not just ideas, but the *very* ideas I needed: general structure, specific organization, detailed evidence. I was about to pass that off—like the check—as an interesting psychological phenomenon, when with my doubts the ideas stopped coming, abruptly as a faucet being turned off.

My feeling is, and it approaches the strength of conviction, that we get help from beyond death. The day Dad died things fell apart around our house—car wouldn't start, water heater rusted out and left us without hot water, blue pen leaked ink all over my shirt. Rob said he had that figured out: "Dad's up there now, and he's trying to help us, and he never was too mechanical." It's true; Dad hasn't made much mechanical contribution. But his help to me has been not just substantial, but personal, the kind of help that only this particular father would know to give this particular son. The satisfying thing—far more than the money, far more than the help on the writing project, was feeling that my Dad was helping, helping in such direct response to my immediate needs it almost insulted me into laughter. I could just see him up there saying, "The boy needs help."

I think he's really with me—I can tell he's watching me; a room will feel warmer because he's in it, loving me. My conviction is that my father was too much alive not to be with us now. And we're more alive because he's with us. His favorite scripture was "I am come that they might have life, and that they might have it more abundantly" (John 10:10). Dad lived that. Before my mission he gave me a blessing that's become better and better as the years have gone by: "I promise that wherever you are and whatever your needs, your loved ones will attend you, and this will be a comfort to you." I feel the comfort. I feel him attending.

Deeper certainty of eternity is a further happy surprise that came for me with the death of my father. Now that he's gone I feel that I have one foot in the grave. But I also feel one foot in eternity. I feel I've a sure friend and ally up there, someone I'm in good with in heaven.

So I've had considerable comfort in my mourning—another positive aspect of my father's good dying. But the comfort, even the sense of his presence, is not enough to take the hurt away. So don't let me kid you about it being okay—life matters too much for us to be facile with each other about death. The consolations are only that: consolation prizes, consolation for serious loss. I'd trade all my comfortings, profound though those have been for me, to have him here right now. I'd trade every eternal intimation of Dad's continuing presence for a single immediate look in those warm brown eyes, one more sound of that rich tenor benediction: "Take care, son. Take care."

DEATH HURTS

My father's death left a hole in my world. What I learned from the death of my father is that death hurts. It hurts something awful, hurts more than when they stick that needle through the bone of your left knee, hurts more than when your high school girlfriend leaves you for a better football player, hurts more than your first lie after baptism, hurts more than anything. Emily Dickinson is absolutely right about death: "Parting is all we know of heaven, and all we need of hell."[2]

The really discouraging thing is that I learned that hard lesson, the lesson that death is unbearably painful, under the best of circumstances. Dad left a lot of himself with us. I see his compassion in my sister Marda, a blend of his kind of honesty and concern that brightens the room she is in just the way he did. I see him in my big brother Robert's lyrical grace of movement, in my little brother Lynn's tough sweetness. And Mom is still with us. I still have Mom to talk to, talk to about Dad. But for all that Dad left, he didn't leave enough to make up for his not being here. Death made clear to me what I could only suspect until I knew it for certain: some people matter so much to us that they continue to matter, matter terribly, even when they are gone. There are people we care for so much that their absence is too much for us. The wonder of this is that even while we are suffering the loss, suffering more than we can handle, we wouldn't have it any other way.

Maybe we need to know that as a people, as Latter-day Saints. Maybe we need to notice those directions in the Doctrine and Covenants that tell us we are supposed to "live together in love, insomuch that thou shalt weep for the loss of them that die" (42:45). Maybe we need to think about Jesus crying at the grave of Lazarus, need to consider that the very Conqueror of death thought it warranted mourning.

Maybe we've pushed death too much into the margins of our

lives so that death no longer exists for us as an immediate physical fact. We have difficulty coming to intimate, personal terms with death because we no longer see it—no longer see our loved ones die, no longer wash and prepare bodies for burial, no longer sit up near the casket through the night, no longer dig and fill graves. We hide from death. We prettify it, falsify it. We displace it to television, where we can watch it safely. We exile death to hospitals, to rest homes, to funeral parlors. We deny ourselves the experience of death—the experience which may be, next to love, the most profound of human experiences. Maybe our avoidance of that greatest of losses is itself a loss.

DEATH CAN TEACH US TO LIVE MORE FULLY

He was so alive, my dad, 5'4" but somehow larger than life. I don't know if every father feels legendary to his children, but mine sure did. I think of his crawling a hundred feet down a pipe at the Spanish Fork sugar factory to clear an obstruction. I think of him swimming out naked in Sevier Lake to retrieve a goose he'd killed with a single BB in the head at a distance farther than I thought that old Winchester would carry. I think of his epic seven breakings of his nose, mostly in fistfights. When I was three he fell heavily past me down wooden stairs in our basement that were so steep I seldom dared to crawl on them. When he pulled the huge splinters out of his palms with the pliers, he didn't even wince.

My father lived so vigorously I can almost hear, even at this distance, echoes of what he used to yell at ball games: "Play it today!" Maybe that's what Dad's death is trying to teach me: play it today. Once you've taken that last step, there's no going back, only on. Life is here. Life is now. The longest eternity will never make that any different. Somebody as smart as God *could* have figured a way to do life without death. He must have done it on purpose, must have given us death for a reason, and maybe that reason is to remind us to live. "Sometimes," as Richard Sewall puts it, "nothing but death will remind us we're alive."[3]

Losing a same-gender parent, particularly a father, a protector, puts a person on the front lines of death. I find myself, in the phalanx of that army, straggling toward the certainty of our dying, hoping for us what Crusaders are said to have wished one another, a good death—not an easy death, and certainly not a happy death—it takes much too miserable a life to make death happy. I wish us a good death. And I pray us the wisdom to confront death honestly enough and soon enough to make a good life. I used to think being "ready for death" meant welcoming it, like Walt Whitman: "Come lovely and soothing death, . . . the sure-enwinding arms of cool-enfolding death."[4] Now I'm not so sure. Maybe those readiest for death are those least willing to go, those most eagerly alive, those who like my father refuse to "go gentle into that good night," who "Rage, rage against the dying of the light."[5]

So we might do well to cling to life as long as possible, even when it comes down to the most painful steps on the steepest parallel bars, to the very end. I think we'd do well to confront death more vigorously, more immediately. My wife and I were consoled considerably by being able to be present when her father died. Reed had stayed with us in our home for the last year and a half of his life, a difficult time for all of us because of serious senility growing out of his Parkinson's disease, itself not a happy way to go. If you value as much as I the courage to hang in there when the going gets rough, you would deeply respect Reed for the way he hung in there his last years. Under circumstances perfectly designed to break a man's spirit, he still put so much into life.

The man just would not quit. He ran away regularly—not so much away from our homes, I'd like to think, as from the frustrations of the disease. We took him to a rest home for a week when we went on vacation, and they put up the rails on his bed to keep him in at night. Reed told us later: "It took me a long time to get up courage to jump out." Even with Parkinson's disease and emphysema and senility, he put so much of himself into living right up to the end. He savored every bite he ate right up to the last bite. He smiled with us the day before he died.

There wasn't much of him left at the end. He couldn't have stood much over 5'5" in tall shoes at his tallest, and he'd shrunk a lot. When Bishop Olpin and I lifted him for the last time from his bed, I was shocked he could weigh so little—he'd seemed so much larger in life. But when we watched him die, I swear he stretched those stubby legs and lifted that emaciated chin as if to rise above the Parkinson's disease and the fogginess of his mind and soar into forever. Watching Reed look upward and outward at the last, seeing him strain his tired body toward where he clearly wanted to go, was immensely reassuring.

It may be helpful to stay as physically close as you can as long as you can, rubbing your father's feet as long as you have the chance. Marda asked the mortician before the funeral if we could dress my father in his temple clothes. Mostly Marda dressed him; I clung to his foot. But there was for me profound personal comfort in rubbing that foot I'd rubbed before, my father's very real and very dead foot, realizing more imminently, in a way I could hold in my hand, that just as surely as this physical father had passed from my life that actual foot would again walk with me. I suspect from the surprising solace of the intimacy of touching my father's dead body that we Latter-day Saints may have dealt better with death as a people in the days when we washed and prepared the bodies, dug and filled in the graves.

Be Prepared Not to Be Prepared

I miss my father most when I least expect to. Dad's birthday, his death anniversary on the eleventh of each month, the Christmas since he died haven't been as hard as I thought they'd be. But that evening I felt that first chill in the air in late August, when you sense fall coming, nearly knocked me over with grief. The next day I remembered Dad's having said that the first feeling of fall was his favorite time of year. Every once in a while a quail will whistle, or a cloud will offer the kind of shapes he used to find animals in, or a sunset will say he is no longer here to enjoy it with me so elementally and undeniably that I can hardly stand his absence. The first time I went to dial his number and realized there is no longer any direct line was the loneliest moment of my life.

And I'm beginning to suspect that Dad's death is not so much the cosmic confrontation with death I've been thinking it was, but just Dad's death. This book is making me aware that we can never say of death, "Been there. Done that." My father's death is different from your mother's death or your neighbor's child's death or your cousin's husband's dying. It's not just that the categories of the experience differ; death is as unique an experience as the particular life it culminates. However much we have been subjected to death, even close hand, we've more to learn about it. Maybe we won't know all there is to know until our own dying.

So whatever preparations we may manage to make for death—mentally, spiritually, emotionally—the main preparation is being prepared to be surprised. There are things about death that can be anticipated, and the more we anticipate the less drastic the impact of death may be. Such practical measures as pre-planning the funeral, writing an obituary before you have to, or anticipating legal and financial challenges may reduce some of the disorientation and ease some of the shock of death.

There are things about death that can be anticipated. What I could never have anticipated is how much I miss the person who is gone. Death hit me in ways I doubt I can ever be ready for. I found myself stunned, even angered, that someone I cared for so much could leave. I was overwhelmed by the hugeness of the loss. My brother Robert is planning to lodge an official complaint with God about death; when he gets to be God he'd like to do away with death altogether. I agree with Robert. But I do feel some gratitude for the major lesson I've learned from death: death helps us learn to value those we love.

Dad was a teacher. He would want us to learn from his death. And our other Father would, too, I think. What I've learned from my father's dying is simple: don't underestimate how much people matter. I thought I was pretty mature at fifty-six, pretty much my own man, pretty much grown beyond being Jess Walker's son. And I thought myself ready for his death—I didn't want him hurting anymore. He fought violently against death, arms bruised from wrist to elbow from the toweling restraints at the last. When he finally went, he went peacefully, and I'm pretty sure it was because he decided to go or nobody would have been able to take him.

The more I see of life, the less I understand of death, and the less I like it. But I understand something of love. I understand something of how much Dad loved life, understand thoroughly now how much—how lastingly and necessarily and profoundly—I love him. I testify to you that there is nothing in this world that matters more than the kind of love we're capable of feeling, the kind of love I feel for my father. My advice as to how to cope with the death of a father is my father's advice, no doubt learned the hard way when his own father died of an aneurism at forty-nine: "Live it up," he told us a thousand times. "Live it up, folks." Faced with the irresistible reality of the death of my father whom I cannot stand to have gone, I say what Dad would say: the way to deal with death, the best way to anticipate the dying of someone you love, is to live more fully.

Notes

1. Judith Viorst, "Summer's End," *If I Were in Charge of the World and Other Worries* (New York: Aladdin Books, 1981), p. 50.
2. Emily Dickinson, "1732," *The Complete Poems of Emily Dickinson*, ed. Thomas H. Johnson (London: Faber and Faber Limited, 1970), p. 703.
3. Richard B. Sewall, "A Sense of the Ending," *The Norton Reader* (New York: W. W. Norton & Company, 1980), p. 648.
4. Walt Whitman, "When Lilacs Last in the Dooryard Bloom'd," *Leaves of Grass* (Philadelphia: Rees Welsh & Co., 1882), p. 260.
5. Dylan Thomas, "Do Not Go Gentle into That Good Night," *The Norton Anthology of English Literature*, 6th ed., vol. 2 (New York: W. W. Norton & Company, 1993), p. 2286.

THE JOY OF MY MOTHER
by Jane Brady

September 22, 1985, my friend Mary and I borrowed her brother's car and drove up to Sundance. It was the first time we had left BYU campus our freshman year and we were looking forward to seeing the fall colors. The leaves blew us away. Having grown up in upstate New York I was well acquainted with trees. So in a sense, driving up the canyon was like going home. Once again, tall, lush pines surrounded me. But unlike New York, where there are hundreds of trees lining every street, these trees I could see past. Instead of limiting my view they were expanding it.

It was a Sunday. As we drove through the canyon and parked the car, Mary and I didn't say a word to each other, didn't talk for nearly the entire day even though we were together for hours. The silence felt perfectly natural at the time, as if we were both so overwhelmed by nature and beauty and love that to speak would ruin the moment, would somehow pierce the tranquility. This wasn't a trip for sharing or analyzing or commenting or trivializing. It was for absorbing until we were filled to overflowing. And the solitude was all the better for having Mary along. There is an added thrill to natural serenity when someone is looking over your shoulder with just as much amazement as you are; it's seeing with four eyes instead of just two.

Jane Brady *lives in an old stone house with her husband, Ken, kids Sam, McKenna, and Emma Jane, and cat Oreo. She alternates teaching Gospel Doctrine with Elder C. Max Caldwell in their American Fork, Utah, ward. She first met Steve Walker ten years ago, while taking his Victorian Literature class at BYU, where her first paper for him was a study of grief in Tennyson's* In Memoriam.

The mountains and trees were almost incandescent. We had come at the perfect time of year. The nights had turned cooler up in the canyon but few trees had lost their leaves. The mountains were just how I like them—a patchwork of color: yellows, greens, all shades of orange, browns, and my favorite, rich, dark red. For a little while we sat near the car because we had the windows unrolled and a George Winston tape in the tape deck. The music, too, was just right—sparse enough that it didn't interfere with concentrated thought, but with a certain angst you could sink your teeth into.

I wandered off by myself and stared at a particular mountain for a long time. The ridge of the mountain caught my attention. Though most of the trees still had their leaves, there were three right up on top that were completely bare. They were missing most of their limbs as well, and I wondered if they were dead. I couldn't take my eyes off the trees, and for several minutes couldn't figure out why. The only reason I could think of was that their death stood out so starkly against all of the lushness. A wave of illumination washed over me as I realized that somewhere deep inside me I had been thinking about Christ and His crucifixion.

Moving out of the house does something to you. I was only three weeks into my freshman year at BYU, but I already felt different. As a result of newfound freedom you realize who you really are. There is no one to rely on but yourself. When you have a thought, it is all yours. When you do something right, only you get the credit. I have always considered myself a spiritual person but I had never before, and have not since, spent so many hours sitting and thinking about who Christ is and what He means to me. Constantly I kept coming back to the powerful feeling of how much I am loved. Part of it was the beauty surrounding me. Part was how happy I was with my new life. But the biggest part was the fact that I felt Christ had lived and died for me, personally, that it was a very individual thing He had done. He knew me and loved me and He would take care of me.

As we descended out of the mountains to the music of a Dan Fogelberg tape, I felt the mantle of the world come back upon me. Actually, I had few responsibilities at that point in my life, mostly just studying and having fun. But the contrast made me realize what a liminal experience I had just had. It was a time out of time. It was as if all time had stopped and space had disappeared and I had just floated. There were no worries or cares in the canyon that day—just earth and sky and me in the middle. It was with reluctance we drove to the dorms, seeing those Provo lights start to twinkle as the last bit of sun went away, knowing the infinite moment was over.

The moment I read the Post-it note on my dorm door I knew. It essentially read, "Jane, Call your dad immediately. It is urgent." Something was wrong with my mom. And what other emergency could there be but . . . ? I wouldn't let myself think it. Maybe she was just hurt.

Making a call Sunday night from the dorms was essentially impossible. "All circuits are busy." I dialed for minutes, then over an hour. The longer it took the more I knew.

Eventually the dorm mother came in. Because I had the receiver up to my ear as I dialed and dialed, Mary had to talk to her for me. But I overheard: "Does she know yet?" There was something outrageous about the fact that this stranger knew an intimate detail about my life—something that would change me forever—while I didn't. I wanted to hit her. Or at least scream at her to go away. But instead of yelling, my body remained completely still. I glanced out of the corner of my eye and saw her scared-little-rabbit look. Why did I have to hear it from her? Why did I have to learn it from a yellow Post-it note on my door? But then, what did I want? To be the one to find her body?

The phone finally rang through. Dad talked very slowly and deliberately. I knew. I knew. The core inside me already knew. But I had been clinging to the hope that she was still alive. When I was twelve she had had a stroke. She had once mentioned—that was the way with Mom: never complaining, just casually mentioning—that she could see white polka dots on everything. That night I begged God not to take her away. Had He heard me? Were these last five years with her just borrowed time? Should I have begged harder, had more faith? Now that I had moved away from home did God think I didn't need her anymore?

"Your mom has passed away." Whatever shred of hope I had

been clinging to snapped. The phone hit the floor. I felt what I never would have expected: physical pain. My chest was crushed. I couldn't breathe with the weight suffocating me. I remember blackness, crying so loud I was screaming. I know some people knocked on the door but Mary made them go away. I was on the floor gasping for air and for light. Then I just lay there in a clump. I remember thinking that I needed a Kleenex, and then realizing that I didn't care, that nothing mattered anymore.

Finally a numb grayness set in. I could hear a slight buzz in my ears. The room was still spinning slightly. My head had come up from under the water and now I felt as if I were floating on a raft. In the middle of the ocean. All alone. In the twilight. I could sense that Mary was still there but she wasn't saying anything.

It was I who realized that the phone was off the hook. I looked over and there it sat on the floor. It was impossible to imagine that my dad would still be there. It must have been more than half an hour since I had spoken to him. But I felt as if I should hang it up. It shouldn't be left dangling. I tentatively moved the receiver to my ear. Breathing. The last thing I remember from that day is anger that he was still there, embarrassment that he had heard me, guilt at what I must have put him through—emptiness.

At the wake I stared at her hands because I couldn't look at her face. Her hands, so familiar, looked different now—those hands, the source of so much warmth and love, now cold and waxy. They were stark white with pink blush artificially applied.

The day of her funeral it rained. At the burial we stood around under black umbrellas, stepped around puddles. We rode in limousines and shook strangers' hands. That afternoon I went down into the basement by myself, to the bed I was sleeping in—not my own room in my own house that I had slept in just three weeks earlier. I could barely see shadows in the darkness, though it was the middle of the day. Again I felt that sense of timelessness. I could have been a baby or an old lady. My mom could be just up the stairs, or, gone.

I got out of my wet clothes and crawled into bed, trying to warm up. The day had gone as I had hoped. Her essence had been represented and honored. Now I could rest.

I've always had cold feet.
But when I was a little girl,
my mother would warm my feet between her legs.
We snuggled together in her dark walnut bed
and I would try to fall asleep without wiggling too much
so that I wouldn't wake her up.
She was like a sun, always warming:
You could walk into a room and just feel her.
I still feel her warmth
but it blows past in a breeze.
I can almost grasp it, but . . .
How I long to sit with her right now.
To lay my head on her lap
and tell her my things.
And feel her heat fill me.
Instead I lie alone in my bed.
Drifting off, feeling dizzy and cold.

As I started to fall asleep the thought drifted through my mind that somehow death is as miraculous as birth: some force is there one second and then gone the next, or the other way around. The significance of that intense power is realized only as the events occur, the veil rent. Death, like birth, is horrible and beautiful at the same time—the ultimate paradox. The woman who had given me life had now been taken in death. My link with the past was gone, everything out of balance. But as I teetered over the brink, looking all that was terrible straight in the eye, my instincts told me to remember, to relish, even to savor.

I've come to the mountains again—back to Provo Canyon. It is twelve years since my mother died. The trees still look the same. But the leaves are different. It's just a few weeks before the time of year she died and the leaves haven't started turning yet. Everything feels green and alive. Everything celebrates life: the running water and buzzing flies, chipmunks scampering, the sun and rich blue sky. Though alone, I feel surrounded, enveloped. Just down the hill is my whole family—Lynn, Dave, Bruce, Carol, Steve, Jim, Donna, and my dad, my children and my husband. And almost even my mom. As I hiked up this mountain a scrap of scripture kept running through my mind: "Whenever two or more of you are gathered in my name, there will I be also."

> I've always had cold feet.
> But when I was a little girl,
> my mother would warm my feet between her legs.
> We snuggled together in her dark walnut bed
> and I would try to fall asleep without wiggling too much
> so that I wouldn't wake her up.
> She was like a sun, always warming:
> You could walk into a room and just feel her.
> I still feel her warmth
> when McKenna wraps her arms around my neck
> and her legs around my waist.
> She squeezes and lets out a little Ungh! for emphasis.
> Or when I hold Emma Jane's check next to mine
> and remember Mom's journal entry written about me,
> written straight to me:
> "Put your baby's cheek next to yours.
> Hum her a little song
> and enjoy feeling how she responds with her whole being
> and loves you back."
> Or the time when Sam came bounding into our room,
> the sky on fire with lightning.
> He was cold and scared
> so I wrapped my arms around him and yes warmed his feet.
> Somewhere along the line
> my feet are warmed too.

Everyone's experience with death is different—even people in the same family often have different reactions to a death. When my mother died I had already left home and was in college, so it wasn't as traumatic as if I had still been living at home. In many ways my mother's death was an uplifting experience in my life. I felt a peace around it, felt it was the best thing for her. Besides, most people expect their parents to die before them. That is the natural way. I can clearly see how other people have had much more traumatic and extensive experience with death than I have.

Yet in some ways, death is death. And death is probably the hardest thing we have to endure in this life. Anything we can do to help each other through is a good thing. I hope the following list may help some people. It describes how my siblings and I have remembered and honored our mother, Marian Joy Crockett Brereton.

Suggestions for Remembering and Honoring a Deceased Mother

Look for things that have been laid in your path to prepare you for this event

Maybe you just read a book about death, maybe you just saw a gift your mother would love. Maybe you, like me, just had a particularly peaceful and spiritual time in your life that was the calm that prepared you for what was to come. Be aware of the Lord's hand in your life and appreciate it.

Have each family member share a favorite memory of her

Not only does this provide the positive experience of sharing, but your mind is refreshed from everyone else's memories. One of the memories I shared with my brothers and sisters was how a month before her death, when we had been vacationing on Lake George, I had taken a moment to savor Mom. Though I had been in a hurry I stopped to walk with her slowly up the many steps from dock to cabin. My mother said she appreciated the company. But the experience had really been a gift for me. After she died I remembered those five minutes as a jewel of a time when I had done precisely the right thing with her.

My brother Jim recalled how important it was to Mom that he go on a mission like our other three brothers had. When he didn't go at nineteen she was disappointed and tried to encourage him to change his mind. For two years she hoped he would still decide to serve a mission. Then when Jim was twenty-one Mom came to Utah on a visit. "She explained that she had something very important to share with me," Jim recalls. "I half expected a lecture, but she tearfully explained that if I never went on a mission she would always love me and always support me. I know this was very hard for her to do. She had lived her life in a way that made it clear what her expectations were for me. This experience had a major impact on my life. My mother loved me even if I made decisions she did not care for. I knew her love for me was unconditional. Several years later, I received my mission call. I hadn't told Mom I had even sent in my papers because I didn't want to disappoint her in case I backed out. What a great opportunity it was to tell her I was going on a mission to Baton Rouge, Louisiana! I remember that she was so overcome she couldn't speak. Her silence spoke volumes."

Cook her favorite food

My mom and her sister Margy made many of their mother's favorite recipes in the week between her death and funeral. My Grandma Crockett was a wonderful cook so the cooking recalled one of the best things about her. Just as they felt at one with their mother by making her famous lemon Grapenut pudding, there has not been one time when I've made my mother's lasagna recipe that I haven't thought of her. I love following the recipe from the exact cookbook she used and seeing the tomato paste spills on the page. Even if your mom isn't a gourmet cook, as mine wasn't, there are always recipes that mean something to you as a family. When I make eggs a la goldenrod every Christmas morning I remember eating the same dish at my big dining room table in New York and looking out the window at the snow. It may even be a nice idea to assemble a cookbook as our Brereton family has, combining in one central location recipes that mean something to you as a family.

Do something hard to honor her

Talk at her funeral. Maybe finish your college education like she always wanted. One difficult thing my brothers Bruce and Dave have done is delve into genealogical research—one of the things my mom cared most about, having served as head stake librarian for many years and having cleared over 30,000 names for temple work. One difficult task which several of my brothers and sisters and I took on was the process of moving her casket from her original burial site in New York to her desired resting place amongst her relatives' graves in Franklin Cemetery. Painful as it was to make arrangements such as securing the plot, arranging the flight for her casket, and providing for transportation to the cemetery, researching and resourcing felt like a posthumous gift I could give to my mother.

Encourage different family members to honor her in their own unique ways

My brother Bruce, a computer professional, wrote Mom's funeral program on the computer. Carol, with a degree in art from BYU, drew the picture on the cover of the program. At the funeral Dave and Carol spoke. If my mother had died at this time in my life I would love to be in charge of setting up a memory table for her to be on display at her viewing. I would include the picture of her when she was two with the red pageboy haircut and the wood carved box that we always used in the Christmas nativity play.

Read the sympathy cards together

Reading the mail, I was amazed at the family friends we heard from and the outpouring of love we felt.

Get together for a family photo shoot

My four brothers and three sisters live all over the country, so when we were together for the funeral we took lots of pictures. We loved one day in particular where we did wacky things such as getting in a pyramid and, as my father *always* insisted, lining up in chronological order from oldest to youngest. It was fun and poignant at the same time—we could imagine Mom making funny faces behind Dad with the camera, just like she used to do to get us to smile for the Christmas card picture.

Have a family testimony meeting

Drawing from each other's strengths and perspectives was particularly needed at this traumatic time. Voicing my own testimony clarified in my mind how I really felt. We had two typed talks Mom had given and we read those too, so even she was participating. My brother Jim got married two years after Mom died, the first time we were together as a family since her death. He was the first child to marry without Mom being there so it was paramount in everyone's mind that she should be. After the wedding the sealer asked Jim and Kelly to bear their testimonies. They both said they knew Mom was in the room with them. I was only nineteen at the time and hadn't gone through the temple, but still remember how sensitive they were to me after the sealing, coming up to me to report in detail what had happened. We all felt it was a tribute to her that our family was worthy to meet in the temple, as we did again the next year when I got married.

Treasure the last time you talked to her and the last experiences you had together

I well remember the last day I talked to Mom, three days before she died. I remember her asking me how my classes were going and if I was eating well. The day after her death I got two letters from her in the mail, and a package the next day.

Take time to grieve as an individual

If possible, set aside other roles you have, such as roles of parent or spouse, to really concentrate on being a son or daughter. I know this was important to some of my brothers and sisters who came alone to the funeral.

Show appreciation to those who give you service

It's nice to keep a running list and write thank-you notes to people who have served you. Because death is a time when people rally together who may have drifted apart, it can be a time of renewed contact. I remember the father of one of my close friends who was away at college making me a cake—it so impressed me that he had gone to the trouble. It was comforting to me to have my mom's friends and Relief Society sisters in the house delivering food and washing the dishes—I hope I thanked them properly.

Do what is most important to you

Perhaps you really want to dedicate the grave. Or maybe what room you sleep in when you come home for the funeral is important to you. Maybe you want to be the one to dress your mother. This is not a time to be passive—the window of opportunity is too small. Listen to yourself and realize what is important to you and don't be shy about making what matters happen.

Make the funeral right for her

How is your mother dressed? Who does her hair and makeup? Is it done in a way that makes her look natural? Our mom had the wrong color of lipstick on at the viewing. It just didn't look like her. We should have brought her tube of lipstick along. Don't feel like you are stepping on the mortuary's toes. They are there to serve you. Have everything just as you and she would want it.

Show respect to your mother by being courteous to all of her friends and those who offer you sympathy

Ask them what their favorite memory of her was or for a word that they think sums up her personality. It was important to me to represent my mother by being courageous and gracious to her friends.

Take time for your siblings

We enjoyed doing things such as asking each other what animals each reminds the others of and analyzing personality types. We dug through the cupboards in the dining room and found old cards and pictures, calling out when we found something of particular interest to a brother or sister. One night we stayed up late telling how everyone met their spouses and had their first kiss.

Sing songs that she loved

The song that most reminds me of my mother is the Primary song "Little Purple Pansies." I also love the memory of her singing "Whenever I Hear the Song of a Bird" and "Popcorn Popping on the Apricot Tree." Every night I sing "You Are My Sunshine" to my little Emma Jane and imagine Mom singing it with me. A few years ago my sister gave me a framed copy of the song "Three Little Fishes." Mom would sit us on her lap, facing her, and sing "Boop, boop, dittum dattum wattum shoo!" tossing our little arms up into the air.

Plant her favorite flower

My mother loved purple flowers. Pansies were the pinnacle—her grandmother had brought them to her in the hospital the day she was born—but violets and lilacs were close seconds. When my sister came home from my mom's funeral, her husband, Mark, had violets and pansies planted in a terra-cotta pot sitting on the front step as a special surprise. My brother Bruce has petunias planted in his backyard to remember Mom. I have purple pansies planted in the flower box outside my kitchen window. We have a tradition of bringing purple flowers to our daughters in the hospital as my brothers and sisters brought lilacs when I was born—violets to McKenna and sterling roses to Emma Jane.

Remember a specific bond you had with her

One of my sisters is proud that she has thick dark brown hair like Mom's. Two of my brothers love genealogy like she did. My brother-in-law taught her how to make stained glass windows. Mom had all eight kids take piano lessons, but my brother Bruce and sister Lynn enjoyed it most—Lynn taught lessons for a long time, and both of them play many of the songs that my mom loved. Bruce's quiet service reminds me of Mom's as he does taxes for the elderly and is involved in Habitat for Humanity and The United Way. Donna keeps alive Mom's legacy of sewing, by sewing and quilting herself as well as teaching her daughters to sew. My mom and I both studied English in college. I also like to remember times Mom and I spent together, one on one. We would go to Utah each summer and stay at her Aunt Geneve's. In the morning we would ride the bus downtown, where she'd spend some of the time working at the library but later we'd meet and go through Temple Square and to all the museums. We'd always eat lunch in the Church Office Building cafeteria and sometimes at the end of the day we'd get ice cream sundaes in ZCMI.

Go to familiar places

Since we all had moved away from home, coming to the house was wonderful—sitting in her study, lying on her bed, rummaging through the attic, walking around the block. And there are other places I feel Mom's presence since her death. She was born in a beautiful farmhouse in Franklin, Idaho. Her ancestors had settled the community, and many of her relatives had lived and died there. I have taken my children up to Franklin nearly every Memorial Day to have a picnic with her great uncle and aunt and to bring them to the Relic Hall which meant so much to her and to the cemetery where she is buried near her ancestors.

Make a book about your mother

Each of the eight children in my family contributed to a book about Mom, and we each have a copy. It includes her patriarchal blessing, her testimony, journal entries, color copies of pictures, and a letter from each of us detailing what she meant to us. I like best the letter that she wrote to Santa when she was five and the mimeographed purple-ink papers that are so typical of her family night ideas.

Make a memory book for a child

This can be especially valuable if you have children that didn't know your mother or were young when she died. It is important to share what she was like and how you feel about her. You could make a book, as inexpensive or elaborate as you wish, that includes pictures of her, favorite sayings, and magazine cutouts of her favorite things: like Reeses Peanut Butter Cups and pansies and lakes in the mountains and playing patty-cake and moon and star goblets and antique furniture. Include a page that describes those things you liked about her, that she was gentle or funny or unselfish.

Make a quilt to represent her life

Perhaps each child in the family could sew a square, or have a family picture transferred onto material. Or maybe one person in the family who enjoys quilting could make a quilt representing different memories or times in Mom's life. Several years after Mom died we gave my dad a quilt with pictures of each of the kids on it. My sister Donna quilted it. I'd love to have some kind of heirloom quilt of my mom, either with material from dresses she wore or other representations of her life.

Dedicate a photo album to her

Include all of your favorite pictures of her in a photo album. It's good to have them all in one place. It's a nice idea to exchange pictures if some siblings have the only copy of particular pictures. My dad gave us all a beautiful eight-by ten-inch photograph of their wedding.

Enlarge a favorite picture of her and put it in a beautiful frame

I keep several black and white pictures of Mom on the top of a bookshelf intermixed with pictures of other relatives. I love the one of her whole family, taken when she was maybe five. She's waving her doll's arm.

Dedicate a journal to her

In a journal, include memories, why you love your mom, what you learned from her, what your feelings were at the funeral, and what compliments people have paid her. This might be written in significantly over the first month and a little more over the first year after the funeral. It will always be a comfort to go back to and read. Carol included a rose from the casket, newspaper clippings, the program, cards she received, and leaves she collected representing each of us eight kids. She even wrote down the names of those who made us lunch the day of Mom's funeral and what china they used.

Read her life history

. . . or write it if it hasn't been written. I loved hearing about Franklin from my mom. I also read her grandfather's history, and asked other relatives to tell me more, especially my Uncle Clair, who was my oldest living ancestor and lived in Franklin until he died earlier this year.

Fulfill an unrealized hope or dream of hers

You could feel a real camaraderie with your mom by accomplishing something she had always wanted to do.

Name a child after her

My first daughter's middle name is Joy, just like my mom's. I've told her from the time she was too young to understand why she was named and how she brings me joy as my mom did. Two of my sisters have also given their daughters the middle name Joy.

Wear her clothes or jewelry

Even if it is just a scarf, something from your mom's wardrobe can remind you of her and make you feel close to her. A son could pick out something special for his wife or daughter. My sister Donna has a dress that was important to her because she remembered Mom wearing it. Carol has mom's fur coat, meaningful to her because she used to dress up in it when she was little. My brother Jim was unmarried when my mom died, but he picked out a favorite pearl necklace to share with his future wife. On my own finger are two small diamonds from my mother's wedding ring that are now in mine. It is important to me that those diamonds were on her hand her entire married life and will be on mine for all my life.

Keep something favorite of hers

Maybe there was a lamp she always read by or a book by an author that she particularly enjoyed that you would like to have. Keep objects near you that remind you of her. I would eventually love to have her wooden jewelry box with roses carved on top. I have a small glass basket that she liked to put flowers in. It is also nice to get gifts back that you had given her.

Talk about her

Relate funny or poignant tales. My mom was such an utterly honest person that it was always hilarious when she would lie to help shock the hiccups out of us by saying she forgot to tell us we had been assigned to give a talk on Sunday. I remember my brother Steve saying how when she was teaching him to drive and he slammed on the brakes and her head hit the windshield that at that moment he realized how desperately he never wanted anything to hurt his mother again. A favorite family story of mine is when Mom cheerfully stayed up all night with Carol to help her finish the stake name badges Carol had promised to do but had procrastinated completing. When the sun came up Mom quietly went to put on her dress and was ready by the door with badges in hand when her ride arrived. She never once reprimanded Carol for her irresponsibility, never uttered a word of complaint, just went off to her all-day meeting.

The great thing about sharing these stories is that they are so representative of Mom. We can all relate to her selflessness towards us, as in the story Jim tells of being eight years old and having perfect attendance at Primary with only one week to go. When he forgot and went to a friend's house to play Mom sent the other kids with another ward member and drove the neighborhood for an hour looking for him. When she finally found him she wasn't upset with his irresponsibility. Instead she was happy to see him, so thrilled that they could still make it in time for the last five minutes of class. Jim still has the Book of Mormon commemorating his perfect attendance for the year. And we all have the memory of a mom who cared about us as individuals.

Celebrate her death day

Several of my brothers and sisters have remarked how fulfilling it has been to go to the temple on the anniversary of her death and perform work for family file names.

My brother Dave encapsulates how all eight of us feel about our mother: "One of the things that we recognize as we become parents ourselves is that raising children requires such a dedication and effort over so many years that despite whatever else we accomplish, our life's greatest work is our children. There is perhaps no greater tribute to a parent than to live as they wanted you to live. Each time we make the right decision, perhaps go out of our way to be compassionate to someone else, accomplish a goal that they taught us was important, teach our own children the values that our parents taught us, we underline the significance of their lives and impact on us. It helps us to remember what they contributed to us as we grieve for them, and to know that their influence can live on if we let it."

HONEYSUCKLE AND IRRIGATION WATER
by Rebecca Clarke

I WILL BE ON YOUR RIGHT HAND
AND ON YOUR LEFT,
AND MY SPIRIT SHALL BE IN YOUR HEARTS,
AND MINE ANGELS ROUND ABOUT YOU,
TO BEAR YOU UP.

—D&C 84:88

MY FIRST DEATH

For me the strangest thing about my first death is that I would never get to see Grandpa alive again. Not even for a little bit. Not ever, until I myself died. It didn't seem right that he couldn't come back and visit for a moment. I bet Grandpa wanted to be at his funeral, to tell one last joke maybe, or wrap his arms tight around Grandma one last time. I felt, at eleven years old, that it was very unfair that when you die you're really gone, even though people might still need you, even though you might need them.

I can remember Grandpa Reed before he got sick, mostly because my mom helped me put layers of plastic wrap over these memories so that they would stay fresh. Consistently came the question, "Do you remember Grandpa before he got sick?" I enjoyed giving my

---

Rebecca Clarke *and her husband, Sam, have one daughter, Eliza Grace. Rebecca is working on her master's degree in marriage and family therapy at Brigham Young University. She loves to take time off from her studies to irrigate and smell the honeysuckle.*

recitation: I must have been five when I followed him to the garage and watched him make a new hole in his belt because he was already getting skinny. I remember how every summer we played in the cold irrigation water that rushed down the back sidewalk, and when it was cold outside we'd play in the living room with the blocks Grandpa made—building towers and guarding them from my brother. At parties we'd stand on the grass, and Grandpa would pitch hula hoops over us like they were horseshoes. I have good memories of Grandpa, Grandpa laughing, Grandpa healthy—such good memories it surprises me that some of my sweetest memories of Grandpa are of him in his sickness.

I was ten when Grandpa came to live with us because Grandma could no longer take care of him. He did things, strange things that sometimes would make us laugh. He called me *Phyllis* or *Ruby* or *Alice*. He swatted at things that weren't there. He talked to the plants. We each had a day to wake up Grandpa and get him ready. My day was Wednesday.

Getting Grandpa to come out of his room was the hardest part. He thought people were after him—even us. He spent a lot of his nighttimes running away. He spent a lot of other nights keeping people out of his room. He would lock himself in during the night by jamming his coatrack (Grandpa called it the "tall man"—they were good friends) between the wall and the door. Once I made it in I hoped that he hadn't relieved himself in his shoes or anywhere else that would have to be cleaned up. If all was well in that area, the only other bad part of the routine was pulling his dentures out of the cup of lukewarm Efferdent, water, and saliva—where they'd soaked all night—to brush them. Shaving Grandpa's face was fun. I had to pull his skin taut or it would just go around in circles under the electric razor. Then I would put Brylcreem on his comb and slick back his white hair, clip his suspenders to his pants that would fall down otherwise, and take him upstairs to eat breakfast. This all had to be done before school.

I did not dread Wednesdays. Not only did I enjoy being around Grandpa and replying to things he said that didn't make sense, I had full faith in the big video in heaven. Grandpa would eventually be able to see all that we had done for him and he would really appreciate it. I was earning my reward. There were significant moments. I fed Grandpa his last meal. It was on Friday. I played choo-choo-train with him and told him to open up his mouth and make a tunnel for the spoon, just like you would with a child. Grandpa was in his blue plaid apron that we used for his mealtimes, and he was more cooperative than usual. After that he lost his appetite.

Grandpa died on Sunday while we kids were at church. His body was gone by the time we got home. Mom and Dad watched him die and said that it was a peaceful experience. They said he just sort of relaxed and let go. But they had to be leaving something out. I always wished I would have been able to see it happen for myself, to get more than the edited version. Would I have been able to see the exact moment? Was it gruesome? Did he scream and yell and try really hard not to die?

As an eleven-year-old, I am sure that I encouraged people to believe that I had no questions or qualms about death. I wish someone would have seen through that. One of the most upsetting things I remember about Grandpa Reed's death was the difficulty I had choreographing my tears. I wanted to show how sad I was, but when people were around it just didn't work like it was supposed to. I felt that this somehow meant that I didn't care for Grandpa as much as I thought I did. This bothered me deeply.

I don't remember much about Grandpa's funeral except that many people kept saying that it was a good thing for us and for Grandpa that he had died. *Would I ever become so calloused?* I desperately wanted them to feel as I did, that death was never never a good thing no matter who it happened to. I didn't want to believe that death made so few ripples in our lives. I didn't want to think that at my passing people might say that it was a good thing I was gone.

The viewing was downright scary for me. I stared at Grandpa long enough in the coffin to swear that I could see him take a very shallow breath every once in a while. I even touched Grandpa's hand in the coffin in a moment of feigned maturity (many of the adults were doing it—kissing him even), and immediately wished that I hadn't. I hadn't guessed how cold he would be, or that he would feel like he was covered with wax. I also didn't know that his eyes wouldn't look quite shut. They had done an autopsy on Grandpa to see why he was sick and even though the cut across his forehead was covered I knew it was there. I couldn't help but imagine Grandpa all skinny and cold in the casket with Frankenstein sutures. I didn't want to think about Grandpa dead, and it was a long time before memories of cool irrigation water rushing down the back sidewalk washed away the nauseating smell of the carnations that surrounded his casket.

My Second Death

Memories of my other grandpa, Grandpa Jess, will always smell like the honeysuckle that grew as tall as his front door. These memories include prickly-whiskered kisses, flowers bigger than I had ever seen, and Grandpa telling us to "Hold onto my pinky." They also include lessons about how to live life. He told us to invest our money. He encouraged us to become educated. Grandpa taught me that life was more worth living than I thought it might be. He said to me one afternoon during a depressing conversation about his failing health, "But it's a good life, Rebecca. Oh, it's a good life."

Grandpa Jess seemed to be on the edge of death for a long time. But he kept on living. He was still there when I came home from my mission, and he even came to my wedding. I began to think he might live forever. Who could imagine his garden without him there to take care of it? Who could imagine Grandma without him?

Friday, on my way home from work, I decided to pay Grandpa Jess a visit. He was in the hospital again. Jess had been in and out of care centers with a broken neck and other problems, but always smiled when he saw me. Grandpa liked to tell stories, and hear stories, and I began to think of what we could talk about that afternoon. As I left the elevator a team of doctors and nurses wheeled Grandpa—on a bed, hooked to tubes and gasping for air—right by me.

I stood and watched from a distance until everyone had left his room. I walked in, not sure what to expect. It was bad. Grandpa was struggling. They had tied him to the bed. His eyes were half shut, and they were jerking around as uncontrollably as his body was. *Oh Grandpa.* I put my hand on his hand and tried to calm him. I told him that I loved him and I squeezed his hand to try and will him to hear me. Then I stood there uselessly and cried into a paper towel. The nurse came in after a little bit and I asked if Grandpa was going to die. Without saying yes she gave me a lengthy description that I didn't want to hear about how Grandpa's body would shut itself down. "How long?" I asked. "It could be hours, or it could be days." I put my cheek against his prickly-whiskered one for the last time.

Sunday morning we got the telephone call. It was one of those times when the phone rings and you immediately know. My husband and I drove to tell my parents, who were staying about an hour away. It was a surrealistic drive, the colors up Provo Canyon too deep and rich for me to have not noticed them before, and the light so bright it almost hurt my eyes. There was a huge bag of tiny shredded paper that we had yet to throw away in the back of our truck; the entire drive a steady stream of it flew out and into the air like confetti. Everything seemed to be celebrating, and Grandpa was all around us.

Grandpa's funeral was an incredible experience. It was profound and moving and fun. It was focused on what Grandpa had instilled in each of us, and on what he might have done if he would have been there. From the pulpit my cousin reminded us of the game called Mousy-Mouse, where we all filled in the rhyming parts of the story that Grandpa typically left out. At the cemetery we could hear Grandpa telling Grandma one last time that he loved her as his sons sang, "I'll Bring You a Daisy a Day," and all of the grandchildren and great-grandchildren handed Grandma a daisy until she had a bouquet she almost could not hold. It was the kind of funeral that I want to have.

My Guardian Angels

My husband and I purchased our first home last summer. It's a small place with a big yard, and one of the things that attracted me to it was the lichen on the front walk from irrigation water—just like Grandpa Reed's. The previous owners had not irrigated for ten years, and their suggestion was to fill in the irrigation ditch and put up a wall. To do that would be unholy, even for one who did not know how to actually irrigate, just how to play in irrigation water.

I was on my hands and knees one morning in the garden,

weeding and dripping with sweat, consumed in worry about all of the money remodeling our little house was taking, and feeling overwhelmed with all the land we had to keep up, when an old man, dressed uncannily like Grandpa Reed in coveralls and a straw hat, drove up on a tractor. I didn't want to have my work or my thoughts interrupted. The man introduced himself and began to tell me how he used to own this land and so on and so forth and I really didn't want to hear all about it right then so I stayed on all fours weeding as he talked to me—he might go on forever and the weeds seemed to be multiplying right before my eyes. Then he asked me if I was going to irrigate. I paused and looked up at him. "I don't know how." "Would you like me to help you do it right now?"

The water rushed down my sidewalk. It flooded the grass and filled the garden. I stepped in it, splashed in it, and sat on the edge of the ditch and was up to my knees in it. It was cold. The old man taught me how to move the flood gate down and how to build little dams out of bricks on the lawn to control the water. He showed me spots where it would be good to put irrigation tubes and spots where I should dig down to make the water flow better. For the first time since his death I felt Grandpa Reed there with me. He was so present I half expected him to be there when I turned around, leaning on a worn-out shovel and laughing at the fact that I would find the work of irrigation so gratifying—or maybe because he was pleased that I enjoyed it half as much as he did. The irrigation water and Grandpa Reed rushed through me and got to my dry spots. It was cold water on a hot, hot day and I was filled. I knew the remodeling would work out. I knew that the garden would eventually get weeded. I knew that buying our home was not a mistake. I knew that Grandpa Reed loved me. I knew that I was loved.

Grandpa Jess did not wait as long as Grandpa Reed did to visit me. I think they wait until you need them. Or until you least expect them. I desperately wanted to pass my graduate statistics class. I had limped along in this class, grasping at what was, for me, never possible to wholly understand. I took my bubble sheet for the final and sat down—knowing that this test would determine to a large extent my future school plans. I started flipping through the pages with the keen awareness that people around me were already confidently fill-ing in their bubbles. Scratch, scratch, scratch. Nothing looked familiar to me.

I got more and more flustered. I couldn't choke on this test. I had to pass this test. I went through all sixty questions and answered three. "Okay, that's a start," I thought. Three out of sixty and guessing on the rest. Could I pass with that? The harder I tried to think, the worse I made things. Then it came to me. Clearly and loud: "You have a good mind, Rebecca. You have a good mind." When I told Grandma about this experience I didn't have to even finish it before she slapped her knee and said, "Jess Walker!" I missed only three.

The closeness of my grandpas' spirits since their deaths is not just a secluded experience. As a marriage and family therapist intern I have the chance to work with people who are grieving the death of a loved one. With these people I often ask the question, "Are there ways in which you are closer to that person now than when they were alive?" I have yet to have a client tell me no. One person expressed it exactly the way it feels to me: "I can feel his smile."

Grandma tells me about how she wants to have Grandpa around, to be able to feel him or hear him. Even in her wanting, she is often left alone. We all are. Both my grandfathers are gone—cold and waxy in those awful coffins. I cannot see them alive again until I myself die. I cannot hold onto Grandpa Jess's pinky or listen to him tell a story. I cannot put the plaid apron on Grandpa Reed to feed him one last meal or stand straight and wait for him to throw the hula hoop over me. But I can feel their smiles in honeysuckle, in my statistics final, and in irrigation water. My angels, my grandfathers, are round about me, bearing me up.

PROPHETIC PERSPECTIVES ON DEATH

by C. Max Caldwell

I remember my own reaction to death as I stood in a cemetery on a wintry day many years ago. My father had passed away a few days before. The day seemed colder than the freezing temperatures; I felt an inward chill created by the waiting space of an open grave. Earlier that day I had watched the casket close over the beloved form of my dear dad. I watched as that terribly impersonal box was lowered into the cold earth and covered by the soil that cut off further visual contact with anything physically connected with him. I realized at that traumatic time that my feelings about death depended upon two things, my memories and my expectations. Perspectives of prophets have helped me confront death, making possible for me more faithful expectations and better memories.

The Book of Mormon features frequent counsel about remembering. Lehi exhorts us to "Remember the words of thy dying father" (2 Nephi 3:25). Memories of Book of Mormon people are constantly recalled to bring about desirable purposes in the lives of the living. Helaman reminded his sons: "I have given unto you the names of our first parents who came out of the land of Jerusalem; and this I have done that when you remember your names ye may remember them;

C. Max Caldwell *lives in American Fork with his wife, Bonnie. They are the parents of five children. He is a retired professor of Church History and Doctrine at BYU. Currently serving as the Gospel Doctrine teacher in his ward, he has served as bishop, president of the Louisiana Baton Rouge Mission, and as a member of the Quorum of Seventy.*

and when ye remember them ye may remember their works; and when ye remember their works ye may know how that it is said, and also written, that they were good" (Helaman 5:6). Perhaps the most notable admonition to remember in the book is the frequently repeated petition embodied in the sacramental prayers: "that they may eat [drink] in remembrance . . . and always remember him" (Moroni 4:3, 5:2). The Book of Mormon makes it clear that feelings and emotions can be created or modified by reflections.

When friends and loved ones are gone, all we have left of them are our memories. Nothing can be done to create additional memories after mortal life ends; we are left to ponder whatever associations and experiences we shared preceding death. As my wife and I have grown older, death has claimed many of our family and close friends. We talk a lot of what life was like when they were still here. We reminisce about our moments together, regardless of how brief or insignificant they may have seemed at the time. Memory cells have a way of recalling some trivial incidents that didn't seem worth remembering—until the person is gone.

Many years ago I visited the boyhood home of David O. McKay in Huntsville, Utah. In an upstairs hallway is a framed picture of two little girls, older sisters of President McKay, who died at the ages of ten and eleven. Above the pictures is inscribed: "Gone, But Not Forgotten." Absence can make the heart grow fonder, but absence without shared memories of previous associations makes the heart sadder.

Parents have a preview of the value of memories when children leave home. As our children have gone away, I have spent a lot of time visiting my memory bank. Always I have wished there had been more deposits, creating a bigger treasury. If memory-making doesn't happen before loved ones leave, nothing can be done to compensate. We are fortunate if we have shared our lives and spent time with those we will miss most. A grieving soul can be soothed with comforting memories.

Even surer solace in the face of death revolves around our expectations. Alma the Younger asks, "Do you look forward with an eye of faith?" (5:15). More fortunate than those with warm memories when death comes are those whose expectations for the future are based upon a correct understanding of the teachings of the Lord about the answer to Job's question, "If a man die shall he live again?" (14:14). It is comforting to know that all mortal beings were first born as spirit children of eternal parents and lived in a premortal world of spirits. Then came mortal birth on this earth, when each spirit personage was clothed in a physical body of flesh and blood. The spirit being continues to live in that body throughout mortality until the event we call death, which is the separation of the spirit from its mortal tabernacle. The body dies and decays, but the spirit person does not, only relocates to another sphere. Alma the Younger declared "the soul could never die" (42:9). Henry Wadsworth Longfellow said the same thing poetically:

> Tell me not, in mournful numbers,
> Life is but an empty dream!—
> For the soul is dead that slumbers,
> And things are not what they seem.
>
> Life is real! Life is earnest!
> And the grave is not its goal;
> Dust thou art, to dust returnest,
> Was not spoken of the soul.[1]

Positive expectations of the life hereafter offer real hope in the face of death. Some people have no expectations concerning a postmortal life and therefore no hope for a continuation of associations with those they love. Though they may possess fond memories of former days, they have no anticipations of further contacts. Latter-day Saints are blessed to have solid hopes of the hereafter through insights from prophets. Prophets not only hold out that hope to us, but offer answers to related questions: Where do spirits go when their bodies die? What might they do there? What conditions exist in the afterlife?

For instance, prophets have provided a number of insights about the habitation of departed spirits. Brigham Young has told us that "When you lay down this tabernacle, where are you going? . . . Into the spirit world. Where is the spirit world? It is right here. . . . Do they go beyond the boundaries of this organized earth? No, they do not."[2]

Joseph Smith saw that "The spirits of the just are exalted to a greater and more glorious work; hence they are blessed in their departure to the world of spirits. . . . They are not far from us, and know and understand our thoughts, feelings, and motions, and are often pained therewith."[3] Alma points out that "the spirits of all men, as soon as they are departed from this mortal body, yea, the spirits of all men, whether they be good or evil, are taken home to that God who gave them life" (40:11).

Orson Pratt clarifies the condition of our state immediately after death: "To go back then, into the presence of God, is to be placed in a condition wherein his presence can be seen. It does not mean, in all cases, that people who return into his presence are immediately placed within a few yards or rods, or within a short distance of his person."[4] Heber C. Kimball corroborates Elder Pratt's perspective: "As for my going into the immediate presence of God when I die, I do not expect it, but I expect to go into the world of spirits and associate with my brethren, and preach the Gospel in the spiritual world, and prepare myself in every necessary way to receive my body again."[5]

Other prophets further clarify conditions in the postmortal world to give us more focused hopes of the hereafter. Several speak of two general divisions or conditions in the world of spirits, paradise and spirit prison. Alma says that "the spirits of those who are righteous are received into a state of happiness, which is called paradise, a state of rest, a state of peace, where they shall rest from all their troubles and from all care, and sorrow" (40:12). The Savior specifies who those righteous are: "The whole world lieth in sin, and groaneth under darkness and under the bondage of sin. . . . For whoso cometh not unto me [by repentance and baptism] is under the bondage of sin. . . . And by this you may know the righteous from the wicked" (D&C 84:49, 51, 53). The righteous, then, are those who have made and kept covenants in the Church and kingdom of God. They are celestial spirits living in paradise who will eventually be resurrected into the celestial kingdom (see D&C 76:50–70).

Joseph Fielding Smith described those righteous dead in paradise:

> The righteous, those who have kept the commandments of the Lord . . . are in happiness in paradise. They cease from all this trouble, and trial, and tribulation, and anguish of soul. They are free from all these torments, because they have been true and faithful to their covenants. All spirits of men after death return to the spirit world. There, as I understand it, the righteous—meaning those who have been baptized and who have been faithful—are gathered in one part and all the others in another part of the spirit world.[6]

Some people have been confused by misunderstanding a statement attributed to the Savior. It is recorded that while hanging on the cross Jesus spoke to the thief these words: "To day shalt thou be with me in paradise" (Luke 23:43). Is it possible for an unrighteous thief to become worthy in an instant to occupy a place where covenant keeping people reside in the presence of the Savior? The Prophet Joseph Smith clarified this apparent inconsistency with the following explanation: "King James' translators make it out to say paradise. But what is paradise? It is a modern word: it does not answer at all to the original word that Jesus made use of. . . . There is nothing in the original word in Greek from which this was taken that signifies paradise; but it was—This day thou shalt be with me in the world of spirits."[7]

The other major condition of postmortal spirits is spirit prison. Clearly anyone bound over to an existence in prison is not free. The Savior taught how all can avoid bondage: "If ye continue in my word, then are ye my disciples indeed; And ye shall know the truth, and the truth shall make you free" (John 8:31–32). We know then that those spirits who are consigned to spirit prison are without the blessings and covenants of the gospel. Either they have never been taught the gospel, or they rejected it, or they may have received it once and then failed to abide by what they were taught.

Obviously this grouping must be made up of at least two general classes. The first is honorable people who live good lives by being generous and honest in their dealings with their fellowmen. They include God-fearing people who worship according to their understanding. They are terrestrial spirits, who are presently worthy of an eventual inheritance in the terrestrial kingdom (see D&C

76:71–80). There may be many of these who accept the gospel when it is presented to them. When the vicarious priesthood ordinances are performed for them in earthly temples they are provided with a valid claim upon a celestial inheritance in the kingdom of our Father, thus breaking the bands of spiritual bondage.

Also in the spirit prison are a second group of people, existing in a different dimension. They are wicked people, those characterized as liars, sorcerers, adulterers, and murderers. This group not only suffers the absence of full gospel blessings, but lives in outer darkness-like conditions, or hell, where they suffer for their evil deeds while they await the second resurrection. These are telestial spirits who are being prepared for their resurrection and inheritance in the glory of the telestial kingdom (see D&C 76:89, 101, 103, 106, 112; Revelation 21:8). There are also in this spirit prison sons of perdition who will be resurrected, but will then be cast out permanently into outer darkness, a kingdom without glory (76:30–49).

Prophets not only provide descriptions of postmortal life, they provide insights into what we will do there. President Joseph F. Smith saw a vision of the redemption of the dead in which he learned that when the Savior visited the spirit world following His own death, He "organized his forces and appointed messengers, clothed with power and authority, and commissioned them to go forth and carry the light of the gospel to them that were in darkness, even to all the spirits of men; and thus was the gospel preached to the dead" (D&C 138:30). This was the beginning of the teaching of the gospel to those in the spirit world who were not yet enjoying the privileges of the Lord's covenant people.

President Smith described in his vision who those messengers are: "I beheld that the faithful elders of this dispensation, when they depart from mortal life, continue their labors in the preaching of the gospel of repentance and redemption, through the sacrifice of the Only Begotten Son of God, among those who are in darkness and under the bondage of sin in the great world of the spirits of the dead" (D&C 138:57). If we knew all that is being done in that spirit world, we would likely discover righteous men and women who have completed their mortal existence accomplishing many familiar tasks. Perhaps the Church organization and duties of its members there will not be strange to those who have rendered faithful service here. Many Latter-day Saints, for example, search family history records to connect family relationships and provide temple ordinances for ancestors. It is not uncommon for these researchers to feel they have been helped by unseen sources. Perhaps such help is provided by spirit world inhabitants who are similarly involved in establishing eternal family ties.

Speaking at a funeral service, President Heber J. Grant told of an illuminating experience concerning the spirit world activity of Fera Young following his death in young manhood:

> One of my nearest and dearest friends in boyhood was Horace G. Whitney. Horace had a dream after Fera died in which the two had a conversation. Horace asked him what he was doing and received this reply: "I am here working, Horace, with the wayward boys and girls of the Church, who are drifting away from it, and I am trying to turn their hearts back to the truth. That is my calling, and it is of far greater importance than it would have been for me to remain upon the earth. I have a great influence with them.[8]

President Brigham Young described the need for deceased faithful saints to be engaged in teaching activities for the benefit of those who need to hear the message of the gospel:

> He [Joseph Smith] has just as much labor on hand as I have; he has just as much to do. Father Smith and Carlos and brother Partridge, yes, and every other good Saint, are just as busy in the spirit world as you and I are here. They can see us, but we cannot see them unless our eyes were opened. What are they doing there? They are preaching, preaching all the time, and preparing the way for us to hasten our work in building temples here and elsewhere. . . . They are hurrying to get ready by the time that we are ready, and we are all hurrying to get ready by the time our Elder Brother is ready. . . .
>
> When the faithful Elders, holding this Priesthood, go into the spirit world they carry with them the same power and Priesthood that they had while in the mortal tabernacle. They have got the victory over the power of the enemy here, consequently when they

> leave this world they have perfect control over those evil spirits, and they cannot be buffeted by Satan.[9]

Many among us wonder about the conditions of postmortality even more than about what we will be doing there. What will it feel like after we die? Prophets also provide perspective on life in the spirit world. Brigham Young visualized what his life might be like in the spirit world, describing it as though it had already happened:

> I have passed from a state of sorrow, grief, mourning, woe, misery, pain, anguish and disappointment into a state of existence, where I can enjoy life to the fullest extent as far as that can be done without a body. My spirit is set free, I thirst no more, I want to sleep no more, I hunger no more, I tire no more, I run, I walk, I labor, I go, I come, I do this, I do that, whatever is required of me, nothing like pain or weariness, I am full of life, full of vigor, and I enjoy the presence of my Heavenly Father, by the power of his Spirit.[10]

An inspired statement made by Joseph Smith sheds some light on the conditions of individuals in the spirit world and our relationships with each other: "And that same sociality which exists among us here will exist among us there, only it will be coupled with eternal glory, which glory we do not now enjoy" (D&C 130:2). Joseph F. Smith expands that perspective on our life hereafter:

> What a glorious thought it is, to me at least, and it must be to all who have conceived of the truth or received it in their hearts, that those from whom we have to part here, we will meet again and see as they are. We will meet the same identical being that we associated with here in the flesh—not some other soul, some other being, or the same being in some other form, but the same identity and the same form and likeness, the same person we knew and were associated with in our mortal existence, even to the wounds in the flesh. Not that a person will always be marred by scars, wounds, deformities, defects or infirmities, for these will be removed in their course, in their proper time, according to the merciful providence of God. Deformity will be removed; defects will be eliminated, and men and women shall attain to the perfection of their spirits, to the perfection that God designed in the beginning.

Speaking of his departed Aunt Rachel, President Smith continued, clarifying that our condition there will not be static:

> She will not always remain just as she will appear when she is restored again to life, but she will go on to perfection. Under that law of restoration that God has provided, she will regain her perfection, the perfection of her youth, the perfection of her glory and of her being, until her resurrected body shall assume the exact stature of the spirit that possessed it here in its perfection, and thus we shall see the glorified, redeemed, exalted, perfected Aunt Rachel, mother, sister, saint and daughter of the living God, her identity being unchanged, as a child may grow to manhood or womanhood and still be the same being. [11]

The picture painted by prophets of conditions in the afterlife is profoundly positive. Heber C. Kimball, first counselor to Brigham Young in the first presidency, spoke at the funeral of second counselor Jedediah M. Grant, who died in 1856:

> I went to see him one day last week, and he reached out his hand and shook hands with me. . . .
>
> He raised himself up and talked for about an hour as busily as he could, telling me what he had seen and what he understood. . . .
>
> He said to me, brother Heber, I have been into the spirit world two nights in succession, and, of all the dreads that ever came across me, the worst was to have to again return to my body, though I had to do it. . . . When in the spirit world, I saw the order of righteous men and women; beheld them organized in their several grades, and there appeared to be no obstructions to my vision; I could see every man and woman in their grade and order. I looked to see if there was any disorder there, but there was none; neither could I see any death, nor any darkness, disorder or confusion.
>
> He said that the people he saw were organized in family capacities; and when he looked at them, he saw grade after grade, and all were organized and in perfect harmony. . . .
>
> He saw the righteous gathered together in the spirit world, and there were no wicked spirits among them. He saw his wife; she was the first person that came to him. He saw many that he knew, but

> did not have conversation with any except his wife Caroline. She came to him, and he said that she looked beautiful and had their little child, that died on the Plains, in her arms, and said, "Mr. Grant, here is little Margaret; you know that the wolves ate her up, but it did not hurt her; here she is all right."
>
> "To my astonishment," he said, "when I looked at families there was a deficiency in some, there was a lack, for I saw families that would not be permitted to come and dwell together, because they had not honored their calling here." . . .
>
> He also spoke of the buildings he saw there, remarking that the Lord gave Solomon wisdom and poured gold and silver into his hands that he might display his skill and ability, and said that the temple erected by Solomon was much inferior to the most ordinary buildings he saw in the spirit world.
>
> In regard to gardens, says brother Grant, "I have seen good gardens on this earth, but I never saw any to compare with those that were there. I saw flowers of numerous kinds, and some with fifty to a hundred different colored flowers growing upon one stalk."[12]

There is yet another consolation from death that prophets point to. "For as in Adam all die," Paul wrote, "even so in Christ shall all be made alive" (1 Corinthians 15:22). No one escapes the inherited results of the Fall of Adam. The Fall, which initiated death, provided the blessed opportunity for us to be born here and receive a body. With that privilege came the responsibility to recognize and choose to live by values that have lasting and joyful consequences, or face the consequences of alternative choices. The Fall provided another opportunity as well—we can escape the hazards, sorrows, trials, and tribulations of this mortal existence. Jacob taught that "death hath passed upon all men, to fulfil the merciful plan of the great Creator," necessitating that "there must needs be a power of resurrection, and the resurrection must needs come unto man by reason of the fall" (2 Nephi 9:6). Among the most joyous insights of prophets regarding death is that all spirits who inhabit a body in this life will receive a resurrected body in a life to come. Benjamin Franklin expressed his conviction of a resurrection when he wrote his own epitaph in 1727 or 1728:

> The Body of
> B. Franklin, Printer
> (Like the Cover of an Old Book,
> Its Contents torn Out
> And Stript of its Lettering and Gilding)
> Lies Here, Food for Worms.
> But the Work shall not be Lost;
> For it will (as he Believ'd) Appear once More
> In a New and More Elegant Edition
> Revised and Corrected
> By the Author.

The final consolation we find in the perspectives of prophets on death is the promise of comfort and peace. Sincere and caring friends commonly extend expressions of comfort. Friends often provide meals and lodging, while others voluntarily bear logistical, financial, or other types of burdens in behalf of those who grieve. The very presence of someone who understands can be a source of solace. Death's experience is particularly difficult when we don't get that human solace. Some grieve without mortal efforts to comfort, their mourning neglected by others. Some, like Job, grieve alone, in total absence of any form of benevolent gesture by another human being.

But even under the best of circumstances, the ability to touch tender feelings of a grieving soul with comforting relief and replace anguish with internal peace is not a power delegated exclusively to mortal beings. Those who sincerely look to the Lord for His love at times of bereavement can come to understand why the Holy Ghost is called a Comforter. The Holy Spirit soothing our spirits is the ultimate source of peace. President Heber J. Grant shared an intimate moment in the life of his family that portrayed the capacity of the Lord to adjust and modify feelings at the time of death of a loved one:

> About one hour before my wife died, I called my children into her room and told them that their mother was dying and for them to bid her good-bye. One of the little girls, about twelve years of age, said to me: "Papa, I do not want my mamma to die. I have been with you in the hospital in San Francisco for six months; time and time

again when mamma was in distress you had administered to her and she has been relieved of her pain and quietly gone to sleep. I want you to lay hands upon my mamma and heal her."

I told my little girl that we all had to die sometime, and that I felt assured in my heart that her mother's time had arrived. She and the rest of the children left the room.

I then knelt down by the bed of my wife (who by this time had lost consciousness) and I told the Lord I acknowledged His hand in life, in death, in joy, in sorrow, in prosperity, or adversity. I thanked Him for the knowledge I had that my wife belonged to me for all eternity, that the gospel of Jesus Christ had been restored, that I knew that by the power and authority of the Priesthood here on the earth that I could and would have my wife forever if I were only faithful as she had been. But I told the Lord that I lacked the strength to have my wife die and to have it affect the faith of my little children in the ordinances of the gospel of Jesus Christ; and I supplicated the Lord with all the strength that I possessed, that He would give to that little girl of mine a knowledge that it was His mind and His will that her mamma should die.

Within an hour my wife passed away, and I called the children back into the room. My little boy about five and a half or six years of age was weeping bitterly, and the little girl twelve years of age took him in her arms and said: "Do not weep, do not cry, Heber; since we went out of this room the voice of the Lord from heaven has said to me, 'In the death of your mamma the will of the Lord shall be done.'"

Tell me, my friends, that I do not know that God hears and answers prayers! Tell me that I do not know that in the hour of adversity the Latter-day Saints are comforted and blessed and consoled as no other people are![13]

President Grant provides a prophetic key to accessing heavenly powers to obtain divine peace and be consoled by the God and Father of us all. The prerequisite key that persuaded the young girl to ask her father to bless her mother and inspired President Grant to plead with the Lord for a blessing in behalf of his children, was faith. President Grant and his twelve-year-old daughter possessed faith in the existence and powers of God that made possible the extension of the heavenly influence. President Harold B. Lee dramatically described a well-known moment in biblical history that similarly identifies the key to obtaining heavenly consolation:

> May I now take you to a sacred scene, portraying one whose all seemed to have been slipping from her grasp and let you feel her strength in a fateful hour! Huddled at the foot of the cross was the silent figure of a beautiful middle-aged mother, with shawl drawn tightly about her head and shoulders. Cruelly tormented on the cross was her firstborn son. One can but feebly understand the intensity of the suffering of Mary's mother heart. She now faced in reality the import of old Simeon's doleful prediction as he had blessed this son as a tiny infant child: (He shall be) ". . . a sign which shall be spoken against; Yea, a sword shall pierce through thine own soul also" (Luke 2:34–35).
>
> What was it that sustained her during her tragic ordeal? She knew the reality of an existence beyond mortal life. Had she not conversed with an angel, a messenger of God? She undoubtedly had heard of her son's last recorded prayer before his betrayal, as has been written by John: "And now, O Father," he had prayed, "glorify thou me with thine own self with the glory which I had with thee before the world was." (John 17:5) This sainted mother with bowed head heard his last prayer murmured from the cross through tortured lips: "Father, into thy hands I commend my spirit"; (Luke 23:46) thus inspiring her with resignation and a testimony of reassurance of a reunion shortly with him and with God, her heavenly Father. Heaven is not far removed from him who in deep sorrow looks confidently forward to the glorious day of resurrection. It was a wise man who said, "We cannot banish dangers, but we can banish fears. We must not demean life, by standing in awe of death."
>
> Remember the story of Job. After his torment his wife came to him and said: "(Why don't you) curse God, and die." (Job 2:9)
>
> And in the majesty of his faith, Job said: "I know that my redeemer liveth, and that he shall stand at the latter day upon the earth: And though after my skin worms destroy this body, yet in my flesh shall I see God: Whom I shall see for myself, and mine eyes shall behold, and not another; though my reins be consumed within me" (Job 19:25–27).

> So to you who have lost loved ones, to you who know the pangs of loneliness, some of us have also gone through the fire and understand what it means. We say to you that in the faith that lifts you beyond the sordid trials of the day and points you to the glorious tomorrow that can be yours if you, too, like the prophet Job, can say, "I know that my redeemer lives."
>
> I leave you my blessing, to bring you the peace that can come only from this knowledge and from the witness that you can receive if you will put your trust in your heavenly Father.[14]

Death comes. Grief accompanies. But comfort is found in the satisfying influences of warm memories. And peace is obtained when our expectations of life past death are couched in faith in the prophetically revealed truths of the gospel of Jesus Christ.

NOTES

1. Henry Wadsworth Longfellow, "A Psalm of Life," *One Hundred and One Famous Poems*, ed. Roy J. Cook (Chicago: Contemporary Books, 1977), p. 123.

2. Brigham Young in *Journal of Discourses* 3:326.

3. Joseph Smith, *Teachings of the Prophet Joseph Smith*, comp. Joseph Fielding Smith (Salt Lake City: Deseret Book, 1976), p. 326.

4. Orson Pratt in *Journal of Discourses* 16:365.

5. Heber C. Kimball in *Journal of Discourses* 3:112.

6. Joseph Fielding Smith, *Doctrines of Salvation* (Salt Lake City: Bookcraft, 1955), 2:230.

7. Joseph Smith, *Teachings of the Prophet Joseph Smith*, p. 309.

8. Heber J. Grant, "Comforting Manifestations," *Improvement Era*, February 1931, p. 190.

9. Brigham Young in *Journal of Discourses* 3:370–71.

10. Ibid., 17:142.

11. Joseph F. Smith, *Gospel Doctrine* (Salt Lake City: Deseret Book, 1977), pp. 23–24.

12. Heber C. Kimball in *Journal of Discourses* 4:135–36.

13. Heber J. Grant, *Gospel Standards* (Salt Lake City: *Improvement Era*, 1943), p. 361.

14. Harold B. Lee, from "From the Valley of Despair to the Mountain Peaks of Hope," memorial service address, May 10, 1971.

INDEX

— G —

— H —

— I —

— J —

— K —

— P —

— Q —

— R —

— S —